I0786682

POTUS1

By John Steuber

The Presidency, Politics and Life of George Washington

For more information on *POTUS1,* visit the Instagram account *potus.1* along with the podcast and YouTube channel called *Through The Eyes of George* and the website www.potus1.com.

Dad,

To the hero and friend who taught me the wisdom that I needed to be the man of God that I am today. Thank you for guiding, teaching, and loving me to be the George Washington that my generation needs.

I love you Dad.

Table of Contents:

SHORT CHRONOLOGICAL BIOGRAPHY

Who is POTUS1? George Washington was the Commander in chief of the Continental Army. He signed the Constitution of the United States, and was our first president under the Constitution which he signed. Furthermore, if you abbreviate the first person who held that primary executive office as our first president of the United States it would be POTUS1. Our nation's capital is named after him. Along with his face being on our money. Also one of our states of the United States is named after him as well. There are many streets and monuments to this individual. It seems as though in 2020 that for all the good POTUS1 did, there is a shade or fading of Washington's legacy.

His memory overall shows a person hesitantly accepting public office, knowing that the integrity of his name, family and country are at stake. Many of the Founding Fathers were more educated then POTUS1. But none of them were as respected and revered overall as George Washington. Yes there were other people as president under the Articles of Confederation, which was written before the U.S Constitution. But the complex and chivalrous man known as the first President of the United States, was the person we as an infant nation owe our attitude of gratitude to. He steered the cadence of our infant nation at its most paramount time. Just as tumultuous as Washington's culture was, our times and our culture are not any different today. For all his flaws and upbringing, there is an example of how we can acknowledge the bad and do better, strive to the good and consider the indifferent things of George Washington.

Like in most of Washington's biographies there is a chronological timeline of his life in one way or another. So, without further rambling let's get this biographical timeline over with, and on to the politics part which is why you probably picked up or bought this book.

George Washington was born February 22, 1732 in Westmoreland County, Virginia. In 1746 Lawrence Washington, writes to Mary Ball Washington asking permission for George to enter the Royal Navy. In 1747 George writes down the rules to civility and decent behavior. He travels to Barbados with half-brother Lawrence in 1751. While there George contracts smallpox, which gives him immunity for the rest of his life. Lawrence dies in 1752 and George also joins Fredericksburg Masonic Lodge. He then journeyed to Ohio Valley with Christopher Gist in 1753 to 1754 and delivers a message from British Commander Dinwiddie. George would later write a famous journal on his travels upon his arrival from the Ohio Valley.

  George Washington accidentally started the French and Indian War in 1754. Washington then surrenders Fort Necessity in 1754. The infamous three bullets holes pierce George's coat while also having two horses shot out from under him at the Battle of Monongahela in 1755. On January 6,1759 George marries Martha Dandridge Custis. They were married for forty years. George is appointed commander in chief of the continental army in 1775. Commander Washington lifts the ban on black recruitment and Thomas Paine publishes "Common Sense" in 1776. Also in 1776 Washington is defeated at the battle of Kips Bay and White Plains. But in December, Washington crosses the treacherous Delaware River to defeat Hessians. George was also defeated at Brandywine in 1777. In December of 1777 George and his army arrive at Valley Forge.

The most important solider to train the Continental Army was, (besides George Washington), Prussian, Baron de Steuben, who arrives in Valley Forge to train troops in 1778.

Baron de Steuben is important because before his leadership the majority of the continental army could not shoot well. They were not hygienically clean. And they also could not march well together.

Commander Washington could only do so much to lead the thousands of troops under his command. He needed some help and Steuben was just the person, despite Steuben's supposed gay lifestyle.

 In 1778 the French alliance was signed in Paris. Unthankful and title-seeking for glory, Benedict Arnold is found to have been a traitor in 1779-1780. The following year in 1781 the Siege of Yorktown begins and Cornwallis surrenders. 1782 is the year of the Newburgh attempted mutiny and also Washington establishes the purple heart. The Treaty of Paris grants American independence in 1783. In 1787 George is unanimously elected as Constitutional Convention president. Furthermore in 1787, the final draft of the Constitution is made while the first publication of the "Federalist Papers" are published. The Founders of the United States along with the generations of U.S. citizens and presidents will continually go back to these very important papers. George is unanimously elected as the first president of the United States, (POTUS1), on April 30,1789. Sadly in 1789, George's mother Mary Ball passes away. He loved her very much. Mary Ball was very strict. Who could blame her. Mary Ball's husband, (George's dad), dies when George was a young boy and then George is metaphorically and instantly made the "man of the house".

POTUS1 set many presidential precedents. George was unanimously elected so there was no reason to campaign for votes. In a way you could very vaguely say that George did campaign after elected to gain the trust of the citizens in the infant country.

 Washington wanted to see the newly infant United States. So he set out on a tour of the Northern states in 1789-1790. Famously the 1790 letter to the Hebrew Congregation is written by POTUS1. 1791 marks the passage of the Whiskey Excise Tax and the Whiskey Rebellion in 1794. Also, George tours the Southern states in 1794 as well. The Bill of Rights is ratified in Virginia's action in 1791. George reluctantly and unanimously is re-elected to the office of the president for a second term in 1792.

Fearing all that he and The Founders had fought, died, and would build together would be lost, he accepts the position and goes down in history as the most famous and beloved of all presidents. The Militia Acts are signed in 1792. Wisely George Washington signed into law, the Slave Trade act of 1794 which severely limited U.S. involvement in the international slave trade. Edmond Genet is caught for treason in 1793. 1795 Edmund Randolph is caught colluding with a French government representative to undermine the Jay Treaty of 1794. In 1796 George establishes the navy and military academy. On March 30,1796 George delivers, his response to Congress about the Jay Treaty. On March 4, 1797 was President George Washington's official last day in office as POTUS1. In 1798 George prepares his last will and testament freeing his slaves. John Adams also appoints Washington to command the army with anticipation of war with France. On December 14, 1799 George Washington dies at Mount Vernon from acute tonsillitis. Sadly in 1806 on May 22, his most trusted companion, confidant and love of George's life passed away, his beloved, faithful, wife, Martha. Mrs. Washington was pivotal to the balanced walk of our beloved POTUS1.

With all the laws signed by POTUS1, he only vetoed two of them. The first veto was the Apportionment Bill of April 5, 1792. This bill outlined the amount of representation in the 1790 census. The second bill that he vetoed was on February 28, 1797. This second veto was a bill for trimming the size of the military. Washington vetoed this 1797 bill with the recommendation of Secretary of War James McHenry.

With all this being said here is a list of the majority of laws George Washington passed as our first President of The United States.

A majority of the laws passed under POTUS1 are listed here:

1. 6/1/1789 Time and Manner of Administrating certain oaths (First act of Congress)
2. 7/4/1789 Tariff Act of 1789
3. 11/21/1789 North Carolina received statehood
4. 11/24/1789 Judiciary Act of 1789 (Established the judicial of the United States)
5. 3/26/1790 1st Naturalization Law
6. 5/29/1790 Rhode Island receives statehood
7. 5/31/1790 Copyright Law
8. 7/16/1790 Residence Act (Established Capitol along Potomac River to be called the District of Columbia)
9. 8/4/1790 Funding Act to assume all Revolutionary war debt from states
10. 12/15/1791 Bill of Rights was ratified
11. 2/25/1791 National Bank established
12. 3/3/1791 First revenue law, The Whiskey Tax
13. 3/4/1791 Vermont receives statehood
14. 4/2/1792 Coinage Act
15. 5/8/1792 Militia Act
16. 6/1/1792 Kentucky receives statehood
17. 2/12/1793 Fugitive Slave Act
18. 4/22/1793 Neutrality Acts
19. 3/4/1794 11th Amendment to the Constitution (restricts individuals from suing the states)
20. 3/22/1794 Slave Trade Act (severely limited our involvement in the international slave trade)
21. 3/27/1794 Naval Act (establishes navy)
22. 11/19/1794 Jay Treaty
23. 1/29/1795 2nd Naturalization Act
24. 2/28/1795 2nd Militia Act
25. 10/27/1795 Treaty of San Lorenzo
26. 6/1/1796 Tennessee receives statehood
27. 11/04/1796 Treaty with Tripoli

THROUGH THE EYES OF GEORGE

George Washington said to John Armstrong on March 26, 1781 that "We ought not to look back, unless it is to derive useful lessons from past errors—& for the purpose of profiting by dear bought experience—To enveigh against things that are past & irremediable, is unpleasing—but to steer clear of the shelves & rocks we have struck upon, is the part of wisdom—equally incumbent on political, as other men, who have their own little bark; or that of others to navigate through the intricate paths of life, or the trackless ocean to the haven of secury & rest."

Just because someone does something bad, heinous or egregious, should we negate any good or honorable things that they did and take down all memory of these people? George Washington did many good things and set many great pillars of power with decorum and class. We can look back and see the good, bad and indifferent things George Washington has done and learn from them like he says in the quote above!

 But if we erase George Washington, the Founders and cancel anything we don't like or offends us, where do we say is the beginning or the standard for what we believe, know or trust in? There would not be a beginning or a standard for what we believe, know or what trust in if we delete, cancel, or erase the past. And if we cancel or erase our nation's past how will we know what not to do if we don't know where the error is? As George Washington says "We ought not to look back, unless it is to derive useful lessons from past errors—& for the purpose of profiting by dear bought experience". Let's only look back from our nation's past to learn.

Is human trafficking modern day slavery? Yes it is. When a young women or man is forced to have sex, that is rape and slavery.

When a person is forced to work for little to no money in a grueling environment with no way to escape…that is slavery! Why do some people say you cannot talk about the issue of slavery and understand the despicableness of it unless you're a black or brown American?

No person alive today was born into 18th century slavery. We can have empathy for the horridness of that time in history. What about slavery today? People of all ages are being used in some way for human trafficking. That is slavery in today's culture. The June 2020 U.S. Department of State Trafficking In Persons Report shows some insight as to the severity of this modern day slave trade. Don't you think we should be doing everything we can to stop the millions of people that go missing and forced into sex, labor or human trafficking? OF COURSE!

The White House issued a fact sheet on January 9th 2019 of everything thus far President Trump has done to combat human trafficking. Here is the link to that information. https://www.whitehouse.gov/briefings-statements/president-donald-j-trump-fighting-eradicate-human-trafficking/

 President Trump cares about what is right on the issue of human trafficking, but he doesn't care what the status quo is on that issue. Because He has done more to help on the issue of human trafficking than any other U.S. President thus far.

 No matter what people believe or talk about whether it is Pizzagate, The Podesta emails, Jeffery Epstein, or the Walmart missing children bulletin boards, human trafficking is modern day slavery. Former President Obama thinks that it's modern day slavery as well. And if that triggers you and you think people cannot talk about slavery because they don't look or feel the part then you need to reorganize your priorities on all human life. Because your life matters just like everyone else's.

On September 25, 2012 Obama made a speech about this very topic for a Clinton Global Initiative event:

"It ought to concern every nation, because it endangers public health and fuels violence and organized crime. I'm talking about the injustice, the outrage, of human trafficking, which must be called by its true name – modern slavery. Now, I do not use that word, "slavery" lightly. It evokes obviously one of the most painful chapters in our nation's history. But around the world, there's no denying the awful reality. When a man, desperate for work, finds himself in a factory or on a fishing boat or in a field, working, toiling, for little or no pay, and beaten if he tries to escape -- that is slavery. When a woman is locked in a sweatshop, or trapped in a home as a domestic servant, alone and abused and incapable of leaving -- that's slavery."

Yes, George Washington owned slaves. Yes that is bad! But if we are going to learn from our past, acknowledge the good, the bad, and the indifferent, how can we grow today if we constantly talk about the past without how to help, fix, or procure a better present? Looking through the eyes of George we can see that people can change for the better. Removing George Washington from history because of past "sins" we only instigate more questions of what was there in that empty gap of history. For it is better to acknowledge the bad and how we've progressed to the better. Don't you think we have had any progress on race in the last 240 plus years? Will we ever move past 18th century slavery in America? There is a dangerous movement to revise history as we know and its called the 1619 project. If we don't know our history, will we ever learn from our mistakes and move forward?

This type of chattel slavery came to the eastern North American shores two to three generations before the Founders were even alive. Around 1617 or 1619. How can you blame someone for starting something when they were not alive when it was instituted?

George Washington and The Founders had nothing to do with the beginnings of chattel slavery. Before any flittering idea of a united group of states was imagined and manifested, the 18th century chattel slavery came from the Dutch and British. These Africans were being sold by the African kings to other countries. To the land we know as the east coast of the United States.

Now this does not excuse how heinous this institution was. It is interesting to note that several slave owners were black Americans as well. That fact does not excuse chattel slavery.

I just wanted to point out that Washington did not start this way of life. It was abolished less than 100 years after the United States was established (1776 to 1865). One thing I think about is how can talking about 18th century slavery help the inner city problem, fatherlessness families, gang violence, school attendance for black or brown Americans? These items in my previous sentence are 21st century issues that need 21st century solutions. You can try to fit a circle in a square peg if you want, but it's never going to work. You will be sitting there a long time. Read Paul Johnson's book "George Washington: The Founding Father" pages 37 & 38 for more information. Don't you think George Washington would want us to change our minds for the better to help and educate others like he did? Don't you think that George Washington would have thought we'd have a solution by now after 240 plus years? There is a difference in talking about the past and learning from it, and talking about that past and staying in that moment. No wonder why people think they are "oppressed" or "slaves" of the 18th century, if that is all some people think or talk about. BUT WE HAVE MADE PROGRESS!

Let's look at the words of someone who came from a less than great upbringing. But did not let "history" or "culture" dictate their future. I am speaking about Dr. Condoleezza Rice. You may be asking yourself, why am I bringing Dr.Rice up? Or you may be saying to yourself "she's an accomplished black American woman who is a traitor to the black community because she does not mirror your world view. I don't recall anyone saying that. NO ONE IS RESPONSIBLE FOR YOUR LIFE BUT YOU. If you rely on any leader in your "community" of race or ethnicity for a job, housing, good family structure, money, you will fail.

In 2010 Dr. Condoleezza Rice said in her memoir "Extraordinary Ordinary People" this about race and 18th century slavery. Now remember Dr. Rice is an accomplished black American woman who did not leave the destiny of her life to the laws, culture and history of the United States. The excerpt from her book on pages 157,158 goes as this:

> "The fact is that race is a constant factor in American life. Yet reacting to every incident, real or imagined, is crippling, tiring and ultimately my counterproductive. I'd grown up in family that believed you might not control your circumstances but you could control your reaction to them. There was no room for being a victim or depending on "the white man" to take care of you. That self sufficiency is the ethos passed down by my ancestors on both sides of the family, and I have internalized it thoroughly. Despite the gross inequities my ancestors faced, there has been progress, and race is today no longer determinative of how far one can go. That said, America is not color blind and likely will never be. Race is ever present, like a birth defect that you learn to live with but can never cure".

How much longer are we going to drag the past into the present with regards to race and 18th century slavery? If we want to improve black and brown American lives, then why don't we investigate the truth of the predominate political party that has been running these inner cites and states? Would new leaders in these cites and states make an impact to reduce the fatherlessness, crime, improve wealth income of these black and brown Americans?

People who constantly bring this up in conversation do not have a focused mindset. They are bitter about something they cannot change, instead of looking to the future that we can try to steer forward. If we don't move forward, sooner or later, some things that were dismantled years ago will eat us alive like a moth to flame or locusts to it's next meal. The United States has accomplished so much more to be remembered for. We defeated the Nazi's, we made electricity, the locomotive, modern appliances and advances in science and technology just to name a few.

Human and sex trafficking still happens today. Children are going missing constantly. Millions of them. Both institutions of sex trafficking and 18th century slavery are terrible but not unequal in the denial of a persons God given free will. The human & sex trafficking that happens today does not have any amendments in the U.S. Constitution to dismantle it. BUT the institution of slavery in the 18th century does, and was torn down. Like a vail from the top down, it was torn asunder, brick by brick to then build a new place for all to live. The Founders of this United States knew that people are imperfect and that the Constitution may at times be imperfect because it was made by people. If you want your world view to make an impact, then win elections and captivate the hearts of the citizens. Where else on earth has a country like the United States that has gotten rid of 18th century slavery in less than 450 years after it was introduced, where as other countries had it for centuries. No where. It was and is still the United States leading the way for freedom and the continuing abolishment of all kinds of slavery.

We have had progress for black and brown Americans as Dr Condoleezza Rice has stated. Also Mary V. Thompson, Researcher at Mount Vernon has spoken of something similar in progress in her George Washington biography from 2019 called "The Only Unavoidable Subject of Regret" on page 329:

"It is a difficult and painful story, but it is also a story of progress and change for the better. The case of George Washington, he changed into someone who saw that slavery was wrong, that freedom was a right of every human, regardless of race".

https://www.mountvernon.org/george-washington/slavery/the-only-unavoidable-subject-of-regret/

https://www.mountvernon.org/george-washington/slavery/washingtons-changing-views-on-slavery/

If you would like to know more about George Washington, slavery and his changing views of that ghastly institution, I suggest reading pages 145-165, in Peter R. Henriques "Realistic Visionary".

Here is a quote from George Washington to Henry Lee on October 31, 1786 about the Constitution:
"I never mean... To possess another slave by purchase; it being among my first wishes to see some plan adopted by which slavery in this country may be abolished by slow, sure, and imperceptible degrees."

So here is a list of just a few things of progress. There are many more. But this book is not an encyclopedia:
- Slave Trade Act of 1794 (signed by George Washington. This law severely limited our involvement in the international slave trade.
- Black soldiers in the American revolution and civil war

- Moratorium on International Slave trade 1808 (completely took us out of International slave trade. No more importation of slaves)
- Paragraph in Draft to the Declaration of Independence (talked about distastefulness and grotesque nature of slavery. But Georgia and South Carolina did not want that in the DOI because slavery was a huge part of there economy So the states compromised knowing they would plant seeds to eventually abolish slavery, 13th amendment)
- 3/5 compromise (counted 3/5th of southern slave population for representation in congress. If the slave states would have 5/5th counted of unfree peoples then the slaves states would have had a stronghold on congress and slavery would likely have lasted into the 20th century.
- JFK executive order 10925 (Affirmative Action)
- 13th Amendment (abolished slavery in 1865)
- 14th Amendment (children born of slaves gained citizenship 1868)
- 15th Amendment (black Americans right to vote)
- 19th Amendment (women's right to vote)
- Civil Rights Act of 1875 (black Americans right to public transportation and accommodations and service on juries)
- Civil Right Act of 1964 (ended segregation in public places and banned employment discrimination)
- Civil Right Act of 1968 (prohibited discrimination concerning the sale, rental, and financing of housing)
- College scholarships today are given to students who are black or native American Indian.
- First black president. (Barrack Hussain Obama, 2008-2016)

Furthermore in all of the previously stated above information, along with the notes and bibliography of this book and the many more things we have done to procure freedom for all, some people still want to act like society owes them something. Even though, those who are complaining about the past blemishes of slavery have never lived in that time period of the 18th century, nor have their grandparents. So why do they complain about something they have never experienced, nor their grandparents experienced? What about thinking for your future, your children, your legacy or your career? Some people leave their destiny, in the hands of history and culture so they can have time to complain. But then those same people wont even have the gall to talk about Human and Sex Trafficking of today. This institution is modern day 18th century slavery. And it does not care who you are or where you come from. It a devilish monster that steals, kills and destroys children and families. It very is bad. Very spiritually wrong. Morally wrong. And it sickens me when people can't think outside themselves and see the progress that Dr. Rice and Mary V. Thompson speak of.

Now I know many of you probably don't like our current president, Donald Trump. That's ok. You are intitled to your opinion of him. BUT you are not entitled to have EVERYONE and I mean everyone in America care about your opinion. If that was true, then we'd all be robots. During the Charlottesville riots, many people who did not agree with President Trump said he was being racist for his response to the incident. I don't think Donald Trump is racist. He called out both sides of this issue and condemned the violence wholly. It seems to me years later that no matter what President Trump does, some people will never agree to disagree, to be amiable to him. That in itself makes a bad recipe for contention and bitterness in your heart. Don't be a sour puss!

For the first time in my voting life, I have never seen a president of the United States deliberately call out the devilish, grotesque institutions of human and sex trafficking on the world stage at the United Nations headquarters when POTUS45 spoke directly to the American people and to the world. I thank and applaud President Donald Trump for standing firming in the virtues that George Washington would expect him to protect in the sanctity of our children.

Here are some sources for the above stated information:

 https://www.whitehouse.gov/briefings-statements/remarks-president-trump-meeting-human-trafficking-southern-border/

https://www.whitehouse.gov/briefings-statements/remarks-president-trump-74th-session-united-nations-general-assembly/

https://abcnews.go.com/Politics/anti-human-trafficking-groups-boycotting-ivanka-trumps-white/story?id=68615924

https://www.cnn.com/2020/01/31/politics/donald-trump-combat-human-trafficking/index.html

Before we move on I would like to talk about the Native American Indian for just a moment. I am not an expert on that topic. BUT if I was asked to comment on that, I would point to Colin G. Calloway's "The Indian World of George Washington" from 2018 on page: 492

> *"The nation-to-nations relationship between the federal government and the Indian tribes today in some ways resembles that which Washington, in many of his writings and some of his policies, aspired to established. But assaults on the rights and resources of Native peoples continue. It remains to be seen if the relationship can ever measure up to Louis Cook's Vison of a chain of friendship too strong ever to be broke, and polished and brightened so pure as never to rust".*

Here is a proclamation from President George Washington about crimes against the Cherokee Nations on December 12, 1792. Remember George Washington was not perfect, and neither are you. He states:

"It highly becomes the honor and good faith of the united States to pursue all legal means for the punishment of those atrocious offenders; I have, therefore, thought fit to issue this my proclamation, hereby exhorting all the citizens of the United States, and requiring all the officers thereof, according to their respective stations, to use their utmost endeavors to bring those offenders to justice."

Also Through The Eyes of George with regards to immigration…

The United States is not perfect and it never will be. But the United States has come a long way since George Washington to improve the implementation of naturalization, immigration and border security. George Washington was not a perfect person nor a perfect President. But some things that a modern United States President does is not new, like wanting some type of naturalization process. Think about this for a moment, would you let anyone into your home?

 Would you let anyone use your belongings without your permission? Do you think anyone should take anything they need from grocery stores because they are hungry without asking first? Why do some businesses, living communities, countries and even our very own homes have locks or walls?

 On a basic level we need to know who is coming in and out of our lives, businesses, and homes. IF we decide that open borders is a good thing along with no immigration policy, then if I were those business owners or government officials I wouldn't be surprised if something harmful, shocking or bad happened to my belongings or property if there was no accountability. George Washington did have an immigration policy. It was tainted in the culture of his time. But there are some parallels to what Washington wanted in immigration to slightly what we have today.

Yes, Washington's culture was different than ours. Of course looking back on past errors you're going to see what could have been done better. Washington was the first president, so how could he know how to do better on immigration? His perspective on who (Naturalization Acts of 1790 & 1795) should be allowed into the country was indifferent at best, in today's cultural eyes. BUT he understood in the simplest form the importance of protecting all your borders, having some kind of naturalization and assimilation process and all those who immigrate to the United States to assimilate. You form your own opinion. But below are the words of POTUS1 on the topic of immigration. You decide for yourself if you agree with protecting all our borders, some type of naturalization and assimilation process.

George's letter to reverend Francis Adrian Vanderkemp on May 28, 1788:
*"I had always hoped that this land might become a safe and agreeable Asylum to the virtuous and persecuted part of mankind, to whatever nation they might belong…Under a good government(which I have no doubt we shall establish this Country certainly promises greater advantages, than almost any other, to persons of moderate property,
who are determined to be sober, industrious and virtuous members of society. And it must not be concealed, that a knowledge that these are the general characteristics of your compatriots would be a principal reason to consider their advent as a valuable acquisition to our infant settlements."*

GW's letter to both Houses of Congress on January 8,1790:
"Various considerations also render it expedient, that the terms on which foreigners may be admitted to the rights of Citizens, should be speedily ascertained by a uniform rule of naturalization."

GW's letter to John Adams on November 15, 1794:
"My opinion with respect to emigration is, that except of useful mechanic's—and some particular descriptions of men—or professions—there is no need of extra encouragement: while the policy, or advantage of its taking place in a body (I mean the settling of them in a body) may be much questioned; for by so doing they retain the language, habits & principles (good or bad) which they bring with them; whereas, by an intermixture with our people, they, or their descendants, get assimilated to our customs, manners and laws: in a word, soon become one people."

I also suggest reading "Washington's Farewell" by John Avlon pages 106-109.

Through The Eyes of George on firearms…
if you leave a gun on a table loaded with a bullet in the chamber will that gun shoot someone? Same goes for a motor vehicle. You turn a car on in the park position on your street where you live, do you think a motor vehicle fatality will happen? What type of deaths do you think occur the most by firearms?
 I'll give you a moment to make up your own statistic while I give you the truth. It's suicide! Now before we get into this topic. Let me remind you that there is little to no information on suicide in George Washington's time and culture. Furthermore, that's not to say that it did not happen. But there was no national database or prevention hotline like we have today. I would lean on the side of this monumental problem being a 21st century issue that cannot be helped with 18th century ideals. But there is a way out of this situation. Here are some statistics…

Suicide, the intentional taking or ending of one own's life account for 60% of deaths with firearms according to the Centers for Disease Control and prevention 2017 study. Suicide is the 10th leading cause of death in America today and approximately 132 people commit suicide everyday. It is not revenge murder or death with firearms involving police either or a viral pandemic. It is suicide. How many deaths by firearms do you think happen on average in today's culture? According to the Pew Research Center and Center for Disease Control and Prevention. Six-in ten U.S. gun deaths came from suicide in 2017.

 YOUR LIFE MATTERS! Every life matters. If that upsets you to hear that then you need to get some Word of God in you, check your moral compass or maybe get some therapy. Or maybe just go live on an island. I do not know. But your life does matter and when people take their own life for one reason or another, it is very sad and very tragic. It's interesting to me the people who are strong proponents of gun control or who are against the second amendment do not talk much about suicide with firearms. A gun will not start shooting and mass killing unless a person picks up the gun.

SO, what can we do to help people with suicidal thoughts or thoughts of depression, sadness, despair or even high levels of chronic stress? There are several possible things that people, or loved ones, or friends, or society could do to help. Of the many things that could be done but not limited to, sharing some Word of God, (John 16:33 & 1John 4:4), or check your moral compass if you don't believe in an intelligent design or god. Or maybe help someone to get some therapy. THE BEST THING WE CAN DO is to be friendly or kind to the people around you, coworkers, family or people you meet. It's impossible to be real genuine friends with everyone. But it is possible to be cordial with those people. AND yes, sometimes tragically people will take their own life with a firearm or by other means.

The suicide prevention hotline is 1-800-273-8255.

The suicide prevention website is
www.suicidepreventionlifeline.org

 Do not forget that YOUR LIFE MATTERS! Every life matters. There are people that care for and love you. Pick up the phone and call someone and tell them what's going on, if you're having thoughts of suicide. If the person you called doesn't pick up the phone call someone else until you find someone that is available. Remember you are loved and people care for you. You are a masterpiece! Everyone has gone through some moments of distress and sadness. And we are here to listen to you!

And remember that the trauma of our souls can not be filled or mended truly in our culture or in a hospital. Any lasting healing we receive comes from the truth of God's Word and from our Heavenly Father.

Whatever your opinion is about firearms, about the second amendment or even about protecting our families, your family and mine along with everyone else's matters and has the right to defend ourselves. If you don't think so, then I suggest you don't complain when someone burglarizes your home or physically harms someone you know. What will you do when some breaks in to your home or hurts your family? Whether it be firearms or anything else legally bought, all families should protect themselves. A firearm is not always the right answer for every family. Maybe a doorbell video recorder or security system. It's your choice for your family to have some type of plan and protection.

Also if anybody and I mean **anybody** gets stopped by the police, why don't you just do that they say? Most of the time people who get shot by police are resisting arrest, have a weapon in their hands, or a past record of violent behavior. Then bad things happen because they won't listen to police. How many unarmed Black, Caucasian, Hispanic, Latino, or Asian Americans get killed by police each year? Not many. Yes thousands of people die a year with firearms. But dozens of Black Americans and White Americans get killed by there own race through gang violence, or domestic disputes. Not police brutality. Show me the raw data on your opinion. And I'll show you the truth. Go to the Reference notes page of this book for the truth. Not my truth, not their truth, or even your truth. But the truth on gun violence. With regards to the 2nd amendment here are some quotes from GW and Founders of the United States.

George Washington's first annual address January 8, 1790:
"A free people ought not only to be armed but disciplined..."

George Washington and Debates of the Massachusetts Convention of February 6, 1788:

"And that the said Constitution be never construed to authorize Congress to infringe the just liberty of the press, or the rights of conscience; or to prevent the people of the United States, who are peaceable citizens, from keeping their own arms; or to raise standing armies, unless necessary for the defense of the United States, or of some one or more of them; or to prevent the people from petitioning, in a peaceable and orderly manner, the federal legislature, for a redress of grievances; or to subject the people to unreasonable searches and seizures of their persons, papers or possessions."

Thomas Jefferson wrote to John Cartwright June 5, 1824:
"the constitutions of most of our states assert that all power is inherent in the people; that they may exercise it by themselves, in all cases to which they think themselves competent, (as in electing their functionaries executive and legislative, and deciding by a jury of themselves, both fact and law, in all judiciary cases in which any fact is involved) or they may act by representatives, freely and equally chosen; that it is their right and duty to be at all times armed; that they are entitled to freedom of person; freedom of religion; freedom of property; and freedom of the press."

George Mason, Virginia Declaration of Rights, June 12 1776:
"That a well-regulated militia, composed of the body of the people, trained to arms, is the proper, natural and safe defense of a free state; that standing armies, in time of peace, should be avoided as dangerous to liberty; and that, in all cases, the military should be under strict subordination to, and governed by, the civil power."

George Mason, referencing advice given to the British Parliament by Pennsylvania governor Sir William Keith, The Debates in the Several State Conventions on the Adoption of the Federal Constitution, June 14, 1788:
"To disarm the people...[i]s the most effectual way to enslave them"

George Mason also addressed the Virginia Ratifying Convention, June 4, 1788: *"I ask who are the militia? They consist now of the whole people, except a few public officers."*

UNPRECEDENTED IMPEACHMENT

George Washington said to Catharine Sawbridge Macaulay Graham in January 9, 1790:
> "I walk on untrodden ground. There is scarcely any action, whose motives may not be subject to a double interpation. There is scarcely any part of my conduct wch may not hearafter be drawn into precedent."

One thing to note is that Washington was big on not having entanglements with foreign alliances. IF he were alive today, I believe with all that Israel has gone through, the USA's and Israel's relationship would possibly be what Washington would have wanted to see. For each nation having a separate relationship with the United States and not entangled with a worldly governing body. Are there any relationships what Washington's administration had that would resemble this current relationship we have with Israel? We tried to have peace with the British after the war but people kept entangling themselves in our business, not minding theirs. Today we have a peaceful and harmonious relationship with the British.

On November 19, 1794 representatives of the United States and Great Britain signed the Jay Treaty. This agreement sought to settle outstanding issues between the two countries that had been left unresolved since American independence. The treaty proved unpopular with the American public but did accomplish the goal of maintaining peace between the two nations and preserving U.S. neutrality.

The embroiled, contentious relationship between the United States and Britain continued after the Revolutionary War. As a result, three main unresolved issues continued. British exports flooded the new U.S. economy. American exports were held up by British trade restrictions. (1) The British occupation of the USA's northern forts that the British Government had agreed to abandon in the 1783 Treaty of Paris.

(2) Also the continuing Native American attacks in these northern areas frustrated Americans. (3)Lastly Great Britain's impressments of American sailors and capture of naval and military supplies to enemy ports on neutral ships induced the two nations to the tipping point of war in the President Washington's two terms in office.

So what was the infant nation to do?

The Jay Treaty as controversial as it was, was the answer to all of these unresolved issues with the British. The French did not particularly enjoy that they just had helped the Americans fight the British, and they were now partners with them. The French government as a whole felt betrayed. The French Revolution which Washington supported at first led to an all out war between Britain and France in 1793. Soon Washington was forced to take sides. The more terrorizing and bloody the French Revolution got with Maximilien Robespierre's minions and the infamous guillotine, the more Washington resented what the French were doing. Even though the Bastille key hung in Mount Vernon's foyer.

 Soon enough there were strong lines of division emerging in the United States between those who supported the French and those who supported the British. In Washington's cabinet the divide could not be more palpable like a strong perfume. Secretary of the Treasury Alexander Hamilton supported the British while Washington's Secretary of State, Thomas Jefferson supported the French. President George Washington knew a second war with the British would obliterate the infant United States. So GW sided with Hamilton and sent his fiercely loyal pro-British Chief Justice John Jay to negotiate with the British Government.

It was unusual to have someone who was not already a statesmen represent the United States, who already had a job as a chief judge of a country. Kind of like how the Democrats in 2019 of the U.S. Congress had questions about President Trump having his fiercely loyal lawyer (Rudy Giuliani) represent Trump and the United States overseas.

 In either case if YOU, were president and there was something that was of the utmost concern for you and the country, like a second war with Great Britain in 1790's, who would you want representing the country?

You would want a hippopotamus and a lion, which by the way both of these animals are very fierce. Don't believe me look it up! Which is what Rudy Giuliani and John Jay were for the presidents they served. Anyway, John Jay went to Hamilton for advice on the treaty. Imagine going to war again with the same country literally right after you've just wrapped up a previous war. Oh yeah we did do that (World War I & II). President Washington most likely would have wanted to prevent that, at all costs.

John Jay's only significant leverage in the negotiations was the threat that the United States would join the Danish and the Swedish governments in defending their neutral status and resisting British seizure of their goods by force of military.

The resulting Jay Treaty addressed few U.S. interests. It gave more rights to the British. The Colonists compromised greatly for fear of a second war with the British. The only concessions Jay received was a surrender of the northwestern posts which were already agreed to in 1783, (seems like a mute point on that one). Also Jay received a commerce treaty with the British that granted the United States limited commercial access to the British West Indies. All other unresolved issues, including the Canadian-Maine boundary, compensation for pre-revolutionary debts, and British seizures of American ships, were to be resolved by arbitration. Chief Justice Jay even conceded that the British government could capture U.S. goods bound for France if the British paid for the goods and could confiscate the goods without payment to the French on American ships. I would think this would definitely incite a fire and fury within the French merchants and governing body.

What do you think the American public and Congress at the time in the 1790's thought about everything that I have previously stated about this treaty?

John Jay's Treaty was incredibly unpopular all around. There was infiltration and a "deep state" coup emerging through various groups and key players for the demise and overthrow of the United States. Edmond Genet, a French statesman, was welcomed by the Washington administration. Little did President Washington know that the French were steaming angry to say the least from the Jay Treaty and were plotting to overthrow the United States to dismantle the fresh foundation of liberty that would shape freedom for generations to come.

Genet had two sets of instructions from the French one to appear copasetic and one to overthrow the United States Government by raising armies of people who resented George Washington's administration and give an ultimatum to Washington as well. French ambassador Jean Antoine Joseph Fauchet gave a warrant of arrest and execution for Genet to Edmound Randolph the former Attorney General and current Secretary of State. Genet was swiftly removed. Shortly after this debacle some within Washington's own cabinet, Edmond Randolph, Secretary of State to be exact, was suspected of taking money from a French statesman to impede the fulfillment of the Jay Treaty. Randolph was having dinner at Mount Vernon with GW, Timothy Pickering, the Secretary of War in 1795, and others. Intercepted documents from retiring French ambassador Jean Antoine Joseph Fauchet showed Randolph's betrayal had surfaced to Pickering. Washington excused himself to speak privately with Secretary Pickering. Washington could not believe it. President Washington was as broken as a person could be in a broken trust of betrayal. Later with more evidence Randolph was confronted by President Washington who was asking for an explanation about these bribes. TALK ABOUT COLLUSION with foreign governments. Washington was totally unaware of this. Randolph was let go of this duties as Secretary of State. Timothy Pickering succeeded him and was now the third Secretary of State of the United States.

Can you believe the betrayal that happened to POTUS1? When I started researching George Washington about six years ago I had to read several of his biographies to really start understanding that his presidency was not without conspiracy or controversy. Like every president since and beyond. George Washington was, whether you believe·it or not, divinely chosen with all his good bad and indifferent qualities. GW was quintessential in keeping the country together.

No matter how bleak and tumultuous a situation might be. Remember that God is still on the throne and that Jesus Christ is coming back, (for further reference go to the chapter called *Our Hope).* Those are things that George Washington as an Anglican Christian and Freemason might have thought of in uncertain times.

President Washington understood that as unpopular as the treaty was, and with the undermining of the American experiment, The Jay Treaty was the price of peace with Great Britain. This treaty gave the United States precious time to strengthen the infant nation for any for seeable conflicts. The Jay Treaty whimpered through the Senate on a 20 to 10 vote on June 24, 1795.

How does impeachment of George Washington tie into all of this?

The House of Representatives were shouting that the Senate had the power to advise and consent on treaties that they were forcing the Lower Chamber to appropriate finances for foreign policy with which they did not agree with. Seem familiar in today's political culture? Nothing is new under the sun. Politics will always be the same discussions with a different wrapping paper. In March 1796 Edward Livingston introduced a resolution calling on Washington and Jay with other relevant documents to be handed over for review before the Lower Chamber would appropriate money for the Jay Treaty.

President Washington gave everything the House of Representatives wanted. But cited executive privilege on a few items of privacy. There was a concern that a dangerous precedent would be set. Does a president have a right to privacy?

Everyone has a right to privacy especially when the President of the United Sates cites executive privilege. It should be respected like it was for President Washington. GW sent a response to this request for more papers and information on March 30,1796. The House of Representatives bolstered every lever of power they had short of impeaching President Washington.

George Washington is known at times for his calm and inviting demeanor. The President's response was anything but calm. Below is the excerpt from Washington taunting the Lower Chamber into impeaching him on March 30, 1796:

"It does not occur, that the inspection of the papers asked for can be relative to any purpose under the cognizance of the House of Representatives, except that of an impeachment; which the resolution has not expressed. I repeat, that I have no disposition to withhold any information, which the duty of my station will permit, or the public good will require to be disclosed; and, in fact, all the papers affecting the negociation with Great Britain were laid before the Senate, when the treaty itself was communicated for their consideration and advice." President Washington's full response to the stubborn House of Representatives is printed below:

"To the United States House of Representatives

United States March 30th 1796.

Gentlemen of the House of Representatives.

With the utmost attention, I have considered your resolution of the twenty fourth instant, requesting me to lay before your House, a copy of the instructions to the Minister of the United States, who negociated the treaty with the king of Great Britain, together with the correspondence and other documents relative to that treaty, excepting such of the said papers, as any existing negociation may render improper to be disclosed.

In deliberating upon this subject, it was impossible for me to lose sight of the principle, which some have avowed in its discussion, or to avoid extending my views to the consequences, which must flow from the admission of that principle.

I trust, that no part of my conduct has ever indicated a disposition to withhold any information, which the constitution has enjoined upon the President, as a duty, to give, or which could be required of him by either House of Congress, as a right; and with truth, I affirm, that it has been, as it will continue to be, while I have the honor to preside in the government, my constant endeavor to harmonize with the other branches thereof; so far as the trust, delegated to me by the people of the United States, and my sense of the obligation it imposes "to preserve, protect and defend the Constitution," will permit.

The nature of foreign negociations requires caution; and their success must often depend on secrecy: and even when brought to a conclusion, a full disclosure of all the measures, demands, or eventual concessions, which may have been proposed or contemplated, would be deemed impolitic; for this might have a pernicious influence on future negociations, or produce immediate inconveniences, perhaps danger and mischief, in relation to the other powers. The necessity of such caution and secrecy was one cogent reason for vesting the power of making treaties, in the President, with the advice and consent of the Senate; the principle, on which that body was formed, confining it to a small number of members. To admit, then, a right in the House of Representatives, to demand, and to have, as a matter of course, all the papers respecting a negociation with a foreign power, would be, to establish a dangerous precedent.

It does not occur, that the inspection of the papers asked for can be relative to any purpose under the cognizance of the House of Representatives, except that of an impeachment; which the resolution has not expressed. I repeat, that I have no disposition to withhold any information, which the duty of my station will permit, or the public good will require to be disclosed; and, in fact, all the papers affecting the negociation with Great Britain were laid before the Senate, when the treaty itself was communicated for their consideration and advice.

The course, which the debate has taken, on the resolution of the House, leads to some observations on the mode of making treaties under the constitution of the United States.

Having been a member of the general convention, and knowing the principles, on which, the constitution was formed, I have ever entertained but one opinion on this subject; and from the first establishment of the government, to this moment, my conduct has exemplified that opinion, that the power of making treaties is exclusively vested in the President, by and with the advice and consent of the Senate; provided two thirds of the Senators present concur; and that every treaty so made, and promulgated, thenceforward became the law of the land. It is thus, that the treaty-making power has been understood by foreign nations; and in all the treaties made with them, we have declared, and they have believed, that, when ratified by the President, with the advice and consent of the Senate, they became obligatory. In this construction of the constitution, every House of Representatives has heretofore acquiesced, and, until the present time, not a doubt or suspicion has appeared to my knowledge, that this construction was not the true one. Nay, they have more than acquiesced; for, till now, without controverting the obligation of such treaties, they have made all the requisite provisions for carrying them into effect.

There is also reason to believe, that this construction agrees with the opinion entertained by the State conventions, when they were deliberating on the constitution, especially by those who objected to it; because there was not required, in commercial treaties, the consent of two thirds of the whole number of the members of the Senate, instead of two thirds of the Senators present; and because, in treaties respecting territorial and certain other rights and claims, the concurrence of three fourths of the whole number of the members of both Houses, respectively, was not made necessary.

It is a fact declared by the General Convention, and universally understood, that the constitution of the United States was the result of a spirit of amity and mutual concession. And it is well known, that under this influence, the smaller States were admitted to an equal representation in the Senate, with the larger States; and that this branch of the government was invested with great powers: for, on the equal participation of those powers, the sovereignty and political safety of the smaller States were deemed essentially to depend.

If other proofs than these, and the plain letter of the constitution itself, be necessary to ascertain the point under consideration, they may be found in the journals of the General Convention, which I have deposited in the office of the department of State. In these journals, it will appear, that a proposition was made, "that no treaty should be binding on the United States, which was not ratified by a law": and that the proposition was explicitly rejected.

As, therefore, it is perfectly clear to my understanding, that the assent of the House of Representatives is not n[e]cessary to the validity of a treaty: as the treaty with Great Britain exhibits, in itself, all the objects requiring legislative provision, and on these, the papers called for can throw no light; and as it is essential to the due administration of the government, that the boundaries, fixed by the constitution between the different departments, should be preserved: a just regard to the constitution, and to the duty of my office, under all the circumstances of this case, forbid a compliance with your request."

Go. Washington.

You think that a president's actions do not get double interpretation? Think again. When President Washington cited executive privilege, his fiery opponents became enraged. The opponents of President Trump were emboldened by fear that he would win again as they had a special council investigation with no clear findings of wrong doing and an impeachment trial also with no clear findings of wrong doing when he cited executive privilege.

From the impeachment inquiry beginning on September 24, 2019 to the acquittal on January 31, 2020 President Donald John Trump should have been released from proposed wrong doing. With regret he was not. Say whatever you wish about POTUS45, one thing is for sure, he has taken a lot of heat on his shoulders from all the fiery darts that have been thrown at him. Makes you wonder, does any U.S. president deserve that much scrutiny, and how mentally strong a person would have to be to still fulfill the duties of the executive office.

One more thing, the reason why I am talking about Donald Trump is because he is the current president. If Hillary Clinton would have won in 2016 I would be talking about her instead. So don't get your pants bunched up because I mention Donald Trump.

Besides the French trying to overthrow the infant United States, there were other groups of people outside the emerging United States in the 1700's also trying to overthrow the newly founded government. George Washington talked about a few examples of this is in a letter from G.W. Snyder October 10th and 24th in 1798.

For further insight and understanding on this chapter read "Mr. President" by Harlow Giles Unger published in 2013 on pages 160-169,179-181,185, 211,213,215-21

STATES RIGHTS

George Washington's Farewell Address September 19th 1796: ".. in the opinion of the People, the distribution or modification of the constitutional powers be in any particular wrong, let it be corrected by an amendment in the way which the constitution designates.—But let there be no change by usurpation; for though this, in one instance, may be the instrument of good, it is the customary weapon by which free governments are destroyed.."

You can't get every citizen of a country to agree on everything. And if you think so, what about those "idealistic socialist utopias" that were supposed to work? In every country where communism, Marxism, fascism, socialism has been tried…it failed. Which countries are you speaking of John? I am so glad you asked…Angola, Cambodia, China, Cuba, Nazi Germany, North Korea, Soviet Union, Venezuela, Vietnam, Zimbabwe just to name a few…the idea of the collective rather than the individual, working for the Federal Government has sadly never worked out in favor of it's citizens. So then what do we do? Shall we replace God with government and rely on these bureaucrats for life liberty and the pursuit of happiness? Indubitably not! WE ought to obey God, (our moral compass), rather than mankind.

  What would POTUS1 do? In Edward Lengel's "First Entrepreneur" Washington biography page 249, he writes about Washington saying "In a free society no man can dictate how an economy functions. George Washington never had the power or the desire to do so. Neither as general nor as president did he command prosperity. Men of talent working alongside him-some life long friends and some, alas, eventual enemies-contributed vitally to winning the Revolutionary War, fashioning a Constitution, creating a government, and setting the nation's course."

Never in history has there been a collection of differing states band together to set up a system of government like what we have today in the United States.

The idea of the United States was unique, new and exciting to Washington and to the Founders. Today it continues to be that shining city on a hill!

Should every single citizen of the United States think the same on every topic of life? Is that possible to achieve? Probably not. With topics including but not limited to:
- Defining what a family or marriage is
- Protecting your property and family and loved ones, 2nd amendment
- Conserving the environment
- Human life

In my first book *Through The Eyes of George* I wrote, "As far as I can tell, there is no evidence that George Washington smoked marijuana or pot of any kind. He grew hemp for industrial uses like for rope and canvas sacks but not for getting high." Because we don't know what George exactly did on this current cultural question of pot, we indubitably should NOT extrapolate what Washington did with the hemp he grew. Any other questions should be left up to the state governments because there is nothing specific on this topic of marijuana or pot in the U.S. Constitution. Also why is it a problem to disagree on a group of people who call themselves a family? I would say and most likely George Washington would say that what is innate or natural for a family to be. One man, one woman then children. BUT some people want you to agree that a family can be what ever you want it to be. Two females, two males.. and so forth. In the United States of America you especially have that freedom to choose what you believe is a family. Just because someone doesn't agree with you doesn't mean that you need to be rude and lash out. Being quick to listen and slow to speak and slow to wrath are important tools for understanding where someone is coming from even if you do not agree with them.

People have sex with animals, nature and other family members and they consider that a family to those people. Can everyone agree on everything? Even the origins of the Rainbow from the Christian bible. Can your family agree what's for dinner? No, sometimes you cannot. But you agree to disagree and move on. That's the beauty of the United States. Having the ability to choose a place to live that molds around your beliefs.

We have fifty states and many U.S. Territories. Pick a location that you enjoy to live in. And remember you won't agree with everything that is around you or being passed into law. George Washington didn't either. But you have a right to choose to do as you please in the privacy of your dwelling and home. That is your sanctuary and place of peace. So protect your peace. It would be mighty difficult to get 320 to 330 million people to agree on everything. I mean why would a place that is more cold and tundra feeling than sunny and hot want to have solar panels? And why would it be inappropriate for a family, (however you want to live), not be able to meet an intruder on the property with the same force the intruders are giving to that family?

 Deciding things on a smaller local level with the most microscopic intrusion of federal government will indubitably lead to more peace and prosperity. If you want to change where you live then vote or be the change you want to see in your life and government. In a letter George Washington wrote to Bushrod Washington, his nephew on the November 9, 1787 he said: "The power under the Constitution will always be with the people. It is entrusted for certain defined purposes and for a certain limited period to representatives of their own chusing; and whenever it is exercised contrary to their interests, or not according to their wishes, their Servants can, and undoubtedly will be, recalled. There will not be wanting those who will bring forward complaints of mal-administration whensoever they occur..

Of these things in a government so constituted and guarded as the proposed one is, I can have no idea; and do firmly believe that whilst many ostensible reasons are held out against the adoption of it the true ones are yet behind the Curtain; not being of a nature to appear in open day.
I believe further, supposing these objections to be founded in purity itself that as great evils result from too much jealousy, as from the want of it. And I adduce several of the Constitutions of these States, as proof thereof. No man is a warmer advocate for proper restraints, and wholesome checks in every department of government than I am; but neither my reasoning, nor my experience, has yet been able to discover the propriety of preventing men from doing good, because there is a possibility of their doing evil."

Also George Washington said in a letter to Henry Lee Jr about the direction of government on October 31, 1786…
"Let the reins of government then be braced and held with a steady hand, and every violation of the constitution be reprehended. If defective, let it be amended, but not suffered to be trampled upon whilst it has an existence."

Have we as a nation not matured at all in how we express our difference of opinion on politics or life? Is it still ok to destroy property, kill people and taking things that aren't ours? **NO** it is not ok to do those things. Would you want people to do those things to you, your business you frequent, or people you care about? NO you would not. And if you do, you should reevaluate your priorities…

 Yes, the Boston Tea Party, was a group of people who destroyed the tea that the citizens did not want to pay taxes on, The Townshend Act and The Tea Act before the nation was founded in 1776. Those individuals that were protesting, some rioted against a tyrannical British government and the East India Company. But we as a country have matured, correct?

I'd rather just stick to peaceful protests without the rioting and looting. Well let me tell you some truth about POTUS1 and the immaturity of people in today's culture as well as in GW's time.

So do the citizens of the United States have a right to peacefully protest and assemble? What is the definition of those words and meaning of rioting, violence, looting?

- **Protest-**a statement or action expressing disapproval of or objection to something
- Peaceful- free from disturbance; tranquil, not involving war or violence
- Riot-a violent disturbance of the peace by a crowd
- Looting- steal goods from (a place), typically during a war or riot
- Violence- behavior involving physical force intended to hurt, damage, or kill someone or something
- Mob- a large crowd of people, especially one that is disorderly and intent on causing trouble or violence.

It seems to me that people in today's 2020 culture have forgotten how to read or have never seen a dictionary when they confuse what a peaceful protest is…

President Washington dealt with people during the Whiskey Rebellion who seem eerily like the rioters in 2020 who confuse what in means to peacefully protest and petition from rioting, looting and murder. This has happened in the Democrat run cites of Portland, Baltimore, Chicago, New York City, Seattle, Minneapolis just to name a few…

The Whiskey Rebellion didn't just stir up randomly. There were a series of events that happened to ignite the Whiskey Rebellion. This rebellion essentially was because of the Whiskey Excise Tax. This tax was a new tax on liquor and whiskey spirits and the whiskey stills that produced them. So some of the farmers in western Pennsylvania did not want to pay that tax. Believing they would have their voice heard they were peacefully assembling and protesting under the First Amendment in the Constitution. Which says that "Congress shall make no law abridging the right of people to peacefully assemble to petition the government for redress of grievances"

Soon this peaceful protest moved from being peaceful, to rioting. Now remember our definitions above. You must not forget those definitions. With anything in life, communication is key. And you must communicate and define your terms. Then a civil harmonious conclusion will reside.

So these tax collectors, as their job was, were coming to submit these writs of demand, to those who weren't paying their whiskey excise taxes. Now this is where it gets bad. Rioters who left the "peaceful protest" were at many times tarring and feathering these tax collectors.

Now think about this for a second, yes I said tarring and feathering. Your skin is resilient, but not enough to resist the searing heat or pain of being tarred and feathered. The farmers who did not want to pay their whiskey excise tax resorted to murder and violence. Some of these farmers who did pay their whiskey excise taxes, were not safe either. And some of their property and stills were damaged by these other farmers who wanted these peaceful farmers to side with them.

In this situation these Pennsylvania farmers moved from peacefully assembling and protesting to tar and feathering and then destroying other people's property who were in the same business as them in making whiskey. That doesn't really make sense to me. These reprobate minded people veered way off track from getting their message heard about the Whiskey Excise Tax. President Washington, by his response to the Whiskey Rebellion, would have hoped we would try to be more civil to one another. But looking at the rioting, and at looting, and at the senseless murder in today's culture, I'd say that POTUS1 would be ashamed of the immaturity of those citizens.

Moving on to the conclusion of the Whiskey Rebellion, soon the mob marched on John Neville's house. John Neville was a tax collector and he had been assisting federal marshal David Lennox in the collecting of these writs of demand for not paying taxes.

The citizens who did not pay their taxes were to appear in federal court in Philadelphia. Now during an attempt to serve one of these writs of demand on William Miller. Shots were fired, forcing Neville back to his home in Bower Hill. This mob of people were already over at William Miller's house. They traveled over to John Neville's house wanting him to surrender to the rebels. Shots were fired and one of these rebels was mortally wounded. If they wouldn't have been trying to encroach on John Neville's house none of these people would have been mortally wounded. They had intent to kill and intent to destroy property. James McFarlane, with the rebels came back to John Neville's home in Bower Hill because they had the intention of forcing him to resign his position as tax collector. John Neville's home was being protected by United States Army at this point. As expected because this mob of violent heathens were out for blood, some fighting ensued, some shots were fired and James McFarland was killed.

McFarland, even though he was a rebel and not wanting to pay his taxes he would not have died if he did not encroach on John Neville's home again. Later these rebels burnt down the outlying buildings of John Neville's home.

How does not paying your whiskey excise tax result in murder, rioting, looting? It does not. Any sound renewed minded person can see this was wrong for these rebels to tar and feather these people and burn down their property. When news of this was brought to President George Washington he gave the Pennsylvania governor the opportunity to act. You know states rights!

Doesn't that sound eerily like these rioters in these 2020 cites forcibly going to peoples businesses to get them to side with them or die. The governor of Pennsylvania acted but did not act as quickly as GW would have wanted, to quell the violence, murder and rioting.

 So POTUS1 assembled a militia of states in the surrounding area to come and protect the property and people of that area. When this mob of heathens heard George Washington was coming with a militia of soldiers, the mob disbanded and dispersed as if being thrown into a lake of fire. Gone forever. President Washington to date in 2020 is the only United States president to physically lead a group of soldiers into battle while holding the office as president. Washington didn't want to see this country he had fought so hard for torn apart in its early years. But he knew he had to let things play out before he acted. Other wise people would have called him a dictator or tyrant like today.

Imagine if there was any large crowd or protest in American History. And every single time the President of the United States intervened with the army or forcing the national guard to act, that would be constant chaos. Because I am writing this book in 2020 and Donald Trump is the president then that is who we shall talk about because it is current and relevant to 2020. If that triggers you then…I don't know what to tell you…here's a binky?

If President Trump without respect and permission from the governors and mayors and rule of law, constantly, sent in soldiers to quell the violence, murder, and looting to every single state and city with this issue, there are some that would say Trump is a dictator or tyrant. BUT was President Washington a dictator or tyrant for sending in soldiers to protect the property and people after letting the governor do their job for a while. NO Washington was not. Sooner or later enough is enough.

The Whiskey Rebellion is just one of many examples in George Washington's life that show nothing is new under the sun. It's all just the same show with a different bow.

George Washington said to John Francis Mercer on September 9, 1786:
"It is important ... That the habits of thinking in a free country should inspire caution in those entrusted with its administration, to confine themselves within their respective constitutional spheres; avoiding in the exercise of the powers of one department to encroach upon another."

When considering difference of thought from any government representative or happiness of that representatives constituents, what comes to mind? One should thoroughly examine that it doesn't matter what you look like or clothes you have on. It matters what you do. Any one can flap their stammering lips and sound good. But can you act accordingly?

George Washington said to Lafayette on June 18,1788 on the tranquility of a leader's people:
"It is a wonder to me, there should be found a single monarch, who does not realize that his own glory and felicity must depend on the prosperity and happiness of his People. How easy is it for a sovereign to do that which shall not only immortalize his, name, but attract the blessings of Millions."

Washington also said to Bushrod Washington on January 15,1783:

"Do not conceive that fine Clothes make fine Men, any more than fine feathers make fine Birds—A plain genteel dress is more admired and obtains more credit than lace & embroidery in the Eyes of the judicious & sensible"

George thought and knew it doesn't really matter what you say but what you do in the differences in government, or godly beliefs, religion or politics that really show your character. There will always be difference of thought in the United States and division of some kind when mankind is involved in government. But what disturbed POTUS1 the most was division within groups of Christians.

George Washington also said to Edward Newenham on the 20th of October 1792:
"Of all the animosities which have existed among mankind those which are caused by a difference of sentiment in Religion appear to be the most inveterate and distressing and ought most to be deprecated. I was in hopes that the enlightened & liberal policy which has marked the present age would at least have reconciled Christians of every denomination so far that we should never again see their religious disputes carried to such a pitch as to endanger the peace of Society."

THE INDISPENSABLE MAN
(what we have learned from POTUS1)

George Washington wrote to Jonathan Boucher on July 9, 1771 and said:
"I conceive a knowledge of books is the basis upon which other knowledge is to be built"

George Washington famously said to Boinod & Gaillard on February 18, 1784:
"To encourage Literature & the Arts, is a duty which every good Citizen owes to his Country, & if I could be instrumental in promoting these, and in aiding your endeavours to do the like, it would give me pleasure."

POTUS1 also said about his personal library to Lawrence Lewis on August 4, 1797:
"I have a great many instructive books, on many subjects, as well as amusing ones."

Where do you receive the best advice and then act on it from those words, those examples or individuals? The answer is your moral compass, God's Word, or your academia studies? Where do you go back to for your foundation? Washington though it was important to be educated and virtuous.

Speaking to his nephew, George Washington said to George Steptoe Washington on December 5, 1790:
"To point out the importance of circumspection in your conduct, it may be proper to observe that a good moral character is the first essential in a man(person), and that the habits contracted at your age are generally indelible, and your conduct here may stamp your character through life. It is therefore highly important that you should endeavor not only to be learned but virtuous."

The Founders looked up to George Washington for his class, demeanor and dignity. Young Washington never had a formal education. So he read a lot of books throughout his life. He had more than 1,200 volumes of books in his personal library. Subjects included but not limited to: politics, law, agriculture, literature, geography, and military strategy and history. Here is a website link to the books in Washington's library.

http://www.librarything.com/catalog/GeorgeWashington

Not all, but here is a few of the authors and books George Washington read:
- King James Version Bible
- *Rules of Civility and Decent Behaviour in Company and Conversation* translated by Francis Hawkins. London: S. Griffin, 1668
- Don Quixote by Miguel de Cervantes Saavedra Translated by Tobias Smollett
- Voltaire
- John Locke
- Jonathan Swift
- William Shakespeare
- Mirabeau, Comte Gabriel-Honoré de Riquetti de
- J.B. Bordley
- Batty Langley
- Cincinnatus
- James Macpherson

Many of the other Founders were well read and educated. They read all kinds of books, history and economics before and during the making of the Constitution. POTUS1, through out his life had something the other Founders did not. He genuinely exemplified what it meant in the good, in the bad, and in the indifferent parts of life to have virtue and morality. STOP your negative thinking if you're being negative to yourself. George most likely did that with himself, in the trying difficult decisions he had to make as President. GW was not perfect. And neither are we. He didn't even want to be president. However President Washington manifested the ideals of a changing heart, a family man, and prudence that people still yearn for in a living example today.

Well if I were to pick the correspondence, letter or speech that is the best advice from George Washington I would choose the Farewell Address from September 19, 1796. The reason why I would choose this particular speech is because President Washington talked about many topics and cautioned about copious things that we in the 21st century still talk about today. Those topics include but not limited to:

- National Unity
- Immigration
- Character and Rule of Law
- The Fight Against Factions and Political Parties
- Constitutional integrity
- Debt and Taxes- Fiscal Discipline
- Caution against foreign influence
- Virtue and Godly beliefs
- Good trade, commercial policy
- Education
- America First- Peace through Strength

Most definitely we tackle all of these topics every four years for the presidential election in one way or another. Washington knew these things were pertinent to his time and culture. NOW stop and think for a moment…We do still deal with all of these things listed above and more, in one way or another.

Concluding this chapter, I have put below Washington's Farewell Address on September 19, 1796. You decide for yourself if this speech is timeless and oozing with wisdom!

Furthermore, I have put the salient parts in this quintessential speech in bold type that POTUS1 said many years ago, but still ring true today.

"To the PEOPLE of the UNITED STATES:

UNITED STATES, 19th September, 1796.

FRIENDS and FELLOW-CITIZENS,

THE period for a new election of a Citizen, to administer the executive government of the United States, being not far distant, and the time actually arrived, when your thoughts must be employed in designating the person, who is to be cloathed with that important trust, it appears to me proper, especially as it may conduce to a more distinct expression of the public voice; that I should now apprise you of the resolution I have formed, to decline being considered among the number of those, out of whom a choice is to be made.

I beg you, at the same time, to do me the justice to be assured, that this resolution has not been taken, without a strict regard to all the considerations appertaining to the relation, which binds a dutiful citizen to his country; and that, in withdrawing the tender of service which silence in my situation might imply, I am influenced by no diminution of zeal for your future interest; no deficiency of grateful respect for your past kindness; but am supported by a full conviction that the step is compatible with both.

The acceptance of, and continuance hitherto in the office to which your suffrages have twice called me; have been a uniform sacrifice of inclination to the opinion of duty, and to a deference for what appeared to be your desire. I constantly hoped, that it would have been much earlier in my power, consistently with motives, which I was not at liberty to disregard, to return to that retirement, from which I had been reluctantly drawn.

The strength of my inclination to do this, previous to the last election, had even led to the preparation of an address to declare it to you; but mature reflection on the then perplexed and critical posture of our affairs with foreign nations, and the unanimous advice of persons entitled to my confidence, impelled me to abandon the idea.

I rejoice, that the state of your concerns, external as well as internal, no longer renders the pursuit of inclination incompatible with the sentiment of duty, or propriety; and am persuaded whatever partiality may be retained for my services, that in the present circumstances of our country, you will not disapprove my determination to retire.

The impressions with which I first undertook the arduous trust, were explained on the proper occasion. In the discharge of this trust, I will only say, that I have with good intentions, contributed towards the organization and administration of the government, the best exertions of which a very fallible judgment was capable. Not unconscious, in the out set, of the inferiority of my qualifications, experience in my own eyes, perhaps still more in the eyes of others, has strengthened the motives to diffidence of myself; and every day the encreasing weight of years admonishes me more and more, that the shade of retirement is as necessary to me as it will be welcome. Satisfied that if any circumstances have given peculiar value to my services, they were temporary, I have the consolation to believe, that while choice and prudence invite me to quit the political scene, patriotism does not forbid it.

In looking forward to the moment, which is intended to terminate the career of my public life, my feelings do not permit me to suspend the deep acknowledgement of that debt of gratitude which I owe to my beloved country, for the many honours it has conferred upon me; still more for the stedfast confidence with which it has supported me; and for the opportunities I have thence enjoyed of manifesting my inviolable attachment, by services faithful and persevering, though in usefulness unequal to my zeal.

If benefits have resulted to our country from these services, let it always be remembered to your praise, and as an instructive example in our annals, that under circumstances in which the passions, agitated in every direction, were liable to mislead, amidst appearances sometimes dubious,—vicissitudes of fortune often discouraging,—in situations in which not unfrequently want of success has countenanced the spirit of criticism—the constancy of your support was the essential prop of the efforts, and a guarantee of the plans by which they were effected.—Profoundly penetrated with this idea, I shall carry it with me to my grave, as a strong incitement to unceasing vows that **Heaven may continue to you the choicest tokens of its beneficence—that your union and brotherly affection my be perpetual—that the free constitution, which is the work of your hands, may be sacredly maintained—that its administration in every department may be stamped with wisdom and virtue— that, in fine, the happiness of the people of these States, under the auspices of liberty, may be made complete, by so careful a preservation and so prudent a use of this blessing as will acquire to them the glory of recommending it to the applause, the affection and adoption of every nation which is yet a stranger to it.**

Here, perhaps, I ought to stop. But a solicitude for your welfare, which cannot end but with my life, and the apprehension of danger, natural to that solicitude, urge me on an occasion like the present, to offer to your solemn contemplation, and to recommend to your frequent review, some sentiments; which are the result of much reflection, of no inconsiderable observation, and which appear to me all important to the permanency of your felicity as a People. These will be offered to you with the more freedom, so you can only see in them the disinterested warnings of a parting friend, who can possibly have no personal motive to bias his counsel. Nor can I forget, as an encouragement to it, your indulgent reception of my sentiments on a former and not dissimilar occasion.

Interwoven as is the love of liberty with every ligament of your hearts, no recommendation of mine is necessary to fortify or confirm the attachment. **The unity of Government which constitutes you one people, is also now dear to you. It is justly so; for it is a main pillar in the edifice of your real independence, the support of your tranquility at home, your peace abroad; of your safety; of your prosperity; of that very Liberty which you so highly prize.** But as it is easy to foresee, that from different causes and from different quarters, much pains will be taken, many artifices employed, to weaken in your minds the conviction of this truth; as this is the point in your political fortress against which the batteries of internal and external enemies will be most constantly and actively (though often covertly and insidiously) directed, it is of infinite moment, that you should properly estimate the immense value of your national Union, to your collective and individual happiness; that you should cherish a cordial, habitual and unmoveable attachment to it; accustoming yourselves to think and speak of it as of the Palladium of your political safety and prosperity; watching for its preservation with jealous anxiety; discountenancing whatever may suggest even a suspicion that it can in any event be abandoned; and indignantly frowning upon the first dawning of every attempt to alienate any portion of our country from the rest, or to enfeeble the sacred ties which now link together the various parts.

For this you have every inducement of sympathy and interest. **Citizens by birth or choice, of a common country, that country has a right to concentrate your affections. The name of AMERICAN, which belongs to you, in your national capacity, must always exalt the just pride of Patriotism, more than any appellation derived from local discriminations. With slight shades of difference, you have the same religion, manners, habits, and political principles. You have in a common cause fought and triumphed together; the Independence and Liberty you possess are the work of joint councils, and joint efforts, of common dangers, sufferings and successes.**

But these considerations, however powerfully they address themselves to your sensibility, are greatly outweighed by those which apply more immediately to your interest.—Here every portion of our country finds the most commanding motives for carefully guarding and preserving the Union of the whole.

The *North*, in an unrestrained intercourse with the *South*, protected by the equal laws of a common government, finds in the productions of the latter, great additional resources of maritime and commercial enterprise and precious materials of manufacturing industry.—The *South* in the same intercourse, benefitting by the Agency of the *North*, sees its agriculture grow and its commence expand. Turning partly into its own channels the seamen of the *North*, it finds its particular navigation invigorated;—and while it contributes, in different ways, to nourish and increase the general mass of the national navigation, it looks forward to the protection of a maritime strength, to which itself is unequally adapted.—The *East*, in a like intercourse with the *West*, already finds, and in the progressive improvement of interior communications, by land and water, will more and more find a valuable vent for the commodities which it brings from abroad, or manufactures at home.—The *West* derives from the *East* supplies requisite to its growth and comfort—and what is perhaps of still greater consequence, it must of necessity owe the *secure* enjoyment of

indispensable *outlets* for its own productions to the weight, influence, and the future maritime strength of the Atlantic side of the Union, directed by an indissoluble community of interest as *one nation*.—Any other tenure by which the *West* can hold this essential advantage, whether derived from its own separate strength, or from an apostate and unnatural connection with any foreign power, must be intrinsically precarious.

While then every part of our country thus feels an immediate and particular interest in Union, all the parts combined cannot fail to find in the united mass of means and efforts greater strength, greater resource, proportionably greater security from external danger, a less frequent interruption of their peace by foreign nations;—and what is of inestimable value! they must derive from Union an exemption from those broils and wars between themselves, which so frequently afflict neighbouring countries, not tied together by the same government; which their own rivalships alone would be sufficient to produce, but which opposite foreign alliances, attachments and intrigues would stimulate and imbitter.— Hence likewise they will avoid the necessity of those overgrown military establishments, which under any form of government are inauspicious to liberty, and which are to be regarded as particularly hostile to Republican Liberty; In this sense it is, that your Union ought to be considered as a main prop of your liberty, and that the love of the one ought to endear to you the preservation of the other.

These considerations speak a persuasive language to every reflecting and virtuous mind, and exhibit the continuance of the UNION as a primary object of Patriotic desire—Is there a doubt, whether a common government can embrace so large a sphere?—Let experience solve it. To listen to mere speculation in such a case were criminal. We are authorised to hope that a proper organization of the whole, with the auxiliary agency of governments for the respective subdivisions, will afford a happy issue to the experiment. 'Tis well worth a fair and full experiment. With such powerful and obvious motives to Union, affecting all parts of our country, while experience shall not have demonstrated its impracticability, **there will always be reason to distrust the patriotism of those, who in any quarter may endeavour to weaken its bands.In contemplating the causes which my disturb our Union, it occurs as matter of serious concern, that any ground should have been furnished for characterising parties by *Geographical* discriminations— *Northern* and *Southern—Atlantic* and *Western*; whence designing men may endeavour to excite a belief that there is a real difference of local interests and views. One of the expedients of party to acquire influence, within particular districts, is to misrepresent the opinions and aims of other districts. You cannot shield yourselves too much against the jealousies and heart burnings which spring from these misrepresentations: they tend to render alien to each other those who ought to be bound together by fraternal affection.**

The inhabitants of our western country have lately had a useful lesson on this head: they have seen, in the negociation by the Executive, and in the unanimous ratification by the Senate, of the treaty with Spain, and in the universal satisfaction at that event, throughout the United States, a decisive proof how unfounded were the suspicions propagated among them of a policy in the General Government and in the Atlantic States unfriendly to their interests in regard to the MISSISSIPPI; they have been witnesses to the formation of two treaties, that with Great Britain and that with Spain, which secure to them every thing they could desire, in respect to our foreign relations, towards confirming their prosperity. Will it not be their wisdom to rely for the preservation of these advantages on the UNION by which they were procured? Will they not henceforth be deaf to those advisers, if such there are, who would sever them from their Brethren and connect them with aliens?

To the efficacy and permanency of your Union, a Government for the whole is indispensable—No alliances, however strict, between the parts can be an adequate substitute; they must inevitably experience the infractions and interruptions which all alliances in all times have experienced.

Sensible of this momentous truth, you have improved upon your first essay, by the adoption of a Constitution of Government better calculated than your former for an intimate Union, and for the efficacious management of your common concerns. This Government, the offspring of our own choice, uninfluenced and unawed, adopted upon full investigation and mature deliberation, completely free in its principles, in the distribution of its powers, uniting security with energy, and containing within itself a provision for its own amendment, has a just claim to your confidence and your support. **Respect for its authority, compliance with its laws, acquiescence in its measures, are duties enjoined by the fundamental maxims of true Liberty. The basis of our political systems is the right of the people to make and to alter their Constitutions of Government—But, the Constitution which at any time exists, 'till changed by an explicit and authentic act of the whole people, is sacredly obligatory upon all. The very idea of the power and the right of the people to establish Government presupposes the duty of every individual to obey the established Government.**

All obstructions to the execution of the Laws, all combinations and associations, under whatever plausible character, with the real design to direct, controul, counteract, or awe the regular deliberation and action of the constituted authorities, are destructive of this fundamental principle, and of fatal tendency. They serve to organize faction, to give it an artificial and extraordinary force---to put in the place of the delegated will of the nation, the will of a party, often a small but artful and enterprizing minority of the community; and, according to the alternate triumphs of different parties, to make the public administration the mirror of the ill concerted and incongruous projects of faction, rather than the organ of consistent and wholesome plans digested by common councils, and modified by mutual interests.

However combinations or associations of the above description may now and then answer popular ends, they are likely in the course of time and things, to become potent engines, by which cunning, ambitious and unprincipled men will be enabled to subvert the power of the people, and to usurp for themselves the reigns of government; destroying afterwards the very engines which have lifted them to unjust dominion.

Towards the preservation of your government, and the permanency of your present happy state, it is requisite, not only that you steadily discountenance irregular oppositions to its acknowledged authority, but also that you resist with care the spirit of innovation upon its principles however specious the pretexts.---One method of assault may be to effect in the forms of the constitution alterations which will impair the energy of the system, and thus to undermine what cannot be directly overthrown. In all the changes to which you may be invited, remember that time and habit are at least as necessary to fix the true character of governments, as of other human institutions---that experience is the surest standard, by which to test the real tendency of the existing constitution of a country---that facility in changes upon the credit of mere hypothesis and opinion, exposes to perpetual change, from the endless variety of hypothesis and opinion; and remember, especially, that for the efficient management of your common interests, in a country so extensive as ours, a government of as much vigour as is consistent with the perfect security of liberty, is indispensable.

 Liberty itself will find in such a government, with powers properly distributed and adjusted, its surest guardian. It is, indeed, little else than a name, where the government is too feeble to withstand the enterprises of faction, to confine each member of the society within the limits prescribed by the laws, and to maintain all in the secure and tranquil enjoyment of the rights of person and property.

I have already intimated to you, the danger of parties in the state, with particular reference to the founding of them on geographical discriminations. Let me now take a more comprehensive view, and warn you in the most solemn manner against the baneful effects of the spirit of party, generally.

This spirit, unfortunately, is inseparable from our nature, having its root in the strongest passions of the human mind.—It exists under different shapes in all governments, more of less stifled, controuled, or repressed; but in those of the popular form, it is seen in its greatest rankness and is truly their worst enemy.

The alternate domination of one faction over another; sharpened by the spirit of revenge, natural to party dissention; which in different ages and countries has perpetrated the most horrid enormities, is itself a frightful despotism.—But this leads at length to a more formal and permanent despotism.—The disorders and miseries, which result, gradually incline the minds of men to seek security and repose in the absolute power of an individual: and sooner or later the chief of some prevailing faction more able or more fortunate than his competitors, turns this disposition to the purposes of his own elevation, on the ruins of Public Liberty.

Without looking forward to the extremity of this kind (which nevertheless ought not to be entirely out of sight) the common and continual mischiefs of the spirit of party are sufficient to make it the interest and duty of a wise People to discourage and restrain it.

It serves always to distract the Public Councils and enfeeble the Public Administration. It agitates the Community with ill founded jealousies and false alarms; kindles the animosity of one part against another, foments occasionally riot and insurrection. It opens the door to foreign influence and corruption, which find a facilitated access to the government itself through the channels of party passions. Thus the policy and the will of one country are subjected to the policy and will of another.

There is an opinion that parties in free countries are useful checks upon the administration of the Government, and serve to keep alive the spirit of Liberty. This within certain limits is probably true; and in Governments of a Monarchial cast, Patriotism may look with indulgence, if not with favour upon the spirit of party. But in those of the popular character, in Governments purely elective, it is a spirit not to be encouraged. From their natural tendency, it is certain there will always be enough of that spirit for every salutary purpose. And there being constant danger of excess, the effort ought to be, by force of public opinion, to mitigate and assuage it. A fire not to be quenched; it demands a uniform vigilance to prevent its bursting into a flame, lest, instead of warming it should consume.

It is important likewise, that the habits of thinking in a free country, should inspire caution, in those entrusted with its administration, to confine themselves within their respective constitutional spheres, avoiding in the exercise of the powers of one department to encroach upon another. The spirit of encroachment tends to consolidate the powers of all the departments in one, and thus to create, whatever the form of government, a real despotism.

A just estimate of that love of power, and proneness to abuse it, which predominates in the human heart, is sufficient to satisfy us of the truth of this position. The necessity of reciprocal checks in the exercise of political power; by dividing and distributing it into different depositories, and constituting each the Guardian of the Public Weal against invasions by the others, has been evinced by experiments ancient and modern: some of them in our country and under our own eyes.

To preserve them must be as necessary as to institute them. If, **in the opinion of the People, the distribution or modification of the constitutional powers be in any particular wrong, let it be corrected by an amendment in the way which the constitution designates.—But let there be no change by usurpation; for though this, in one instance, may be the instrument of good, it is the customary weapon by which free governments are destroyed.—The precedent must always greatly overbalance in permanent evil any partial or transient benefit which the use can at any time yield.**

Of all the dispositions and habits which lead to political prosperity, Religion and Morality are indispensable supports.—In vain would that man claim the tribute of Patriotism, who should labour to subvert these great pillars of human happiness, these firmest props of the duties of Men and Citizens.—The mere Politician, equally with the pious man ought to respect and to cherish them.—A volume could not trace all their connections with private and public felicity. Let it simply be asked where is the security for property, for reputation, for life, if the sense of religious obligation *desert* the oaths, which are the instruments of investigation in Courts of Justice? And let us with caution indulge the supposition, that morality can be maintained without religion. Whatever may be conceded to the influence of refined education on minds of peculiar structure; reason and experience both forbid us to expect that national morality can prevail in exclusion of religious principle.

'Tis substantially true, that virtue or morality is a necessary spring of popular government. The rule indeed extends with more or less force to every species of free government. Who that is a sincere friend to it can look with indifference upon attempts to shake the foundation of the fabric?

Promote, then, as an object of primary importance, institutions for the general diffusion of knowledge.—In proportion as the structure of a government gives force to public opinion, it is essential that public opinion should be enlightened.

As a very important source of strength and security cherish public credit. One method of preserving it is to use it as sparingly as possible; avoiding occasions of expence by cultivating peace, but remembering also that timely disbursements to prepare for danger frequently prevent much greater disbursements to repel it; avoiding likewise the accumulation of debt, not only by shunning occasions of expence, but by vigorous exertions in time of peace to discharge the debts which unavoidable wars may have occasioned, not ungenerously throwing upon posterity the burthen which we ourselves ought to bear.—The execution of these maxims belongs to your representatives, but it is necessary that public opinion should cooperate.—To facilitate to them the performance of their duty, it is essential that you should practically bear in mind, that towards the payment of debts there must be Revenue: that to have Revenue there must be taxes; that no taxes can be devised which are not more or less inconvenient and unpleasant; that the intrinsic embarrassment inseparable from the selection of the proper objects (which is always a choice of difficulties) ought to be a decisive motive for a candid construction of the conduct of the government in making it, and for a spirit of acquiescence in the measures for obtaining Revenue which the public exigencies may at any time dictate.

Observe good faith and justice towards all Nations, cultivate peace and harmony with all; Religion and Morality enjoin this conduct; and can it be that good policy does not equally enjoin it? It will be worthy of a free, enlightened, and, at no distant period, a great Nation, to give to mankind the magnanimous and too novel example of a people always guided by an exalted justice and benevolence. Who can doubt that in the course of time and things the fruits of such a plan would richly repay any temporary advantages which might be lost by a steady adherence to it? Can it be, that Providence has not connected the permanent felicity of a Nation with its Virtue? The experiment, at least, is recommended by every sentiment which ennobles human nature. Alas! is it rendered impossible by its vices?

In the execution of such a plan, nothing is more essential than that permanent, inveterate antipathies against particular Nations, and passionate attachments for others should be excluded; and that in place of them just and amicable feelings towards all should be cultivated. The Nation, which indulges towards another an habitual hatred, or an habitual fondness, is in some degree a slave. It is a slave to its animosity or to its affection, either of which is sufficient to lead it astray from its duty and its interest. Antipathy in one nation against another disposes each more readily to offer insult and injury, to lay hold of slight causes of umbrage, and to be haughty and intractable, when accidental or trifling occasions of dispute occur. Hence frequent collisions, obstinate, envenomed and bloody contests. The Nation, prompted by ill will and resentment, sometimes impels to war the Government, contrary to the best calculations of policy. The Government sometimes participates in the national propensity, and adopts through passion what reason would reject; at other times, it makes the animosity of the nation subservient to projects of hostility instigated by pride, ambition and other sinister and pernicious motives. The peace often, sometimes perhaps the liberty, of Nations has been the victim.

So likewise, a passionate attachment of one Nation for another produces a variety of evils. Sympathy for the favourite Nation, facilitating the illusion of an imaginary common interest, in cases where no real common interest exists, and infusing into one the enmities of the other, betrays the former into a participation in the quarrels and wars of the latter, without adequate inducement or justification.

It leads also to concessions to the favourite Nation of privileges denied to others, which is apt doubly to injure the Nation making the concessions; by unnecessarily parting with what ought to have been retained; and by exciting jealousy, ill will, and a disposition to retaliate, in the parties from whom equal privileges are withheld: And it gives to ambitious, corrupted, or deluded citizens (who devote themselves to the favourite nation) facility to betray, or sacrifice the interests of their own country, without odium, sometimes even with popularity; gilding with the appearances of a virtuous sense of obligation a commendable deference for public opinion, or a laudable zeal for public good, the base or foolish compliances of ambition, corruption or infatuation.

As avenues to foreign influence in innumerable ways, such attachments are particularly alarming to the truly enlightened and independent Patriot. How many opportunities do they afford to tamper with domestic factions, to practice the acts of seduction, to mislead public opinion, to influence or awe the Public Councils! Such an attachment of a small or weak, towards a great and powerful nation, dooms the former to be the satellite of the latter. Against the insidious wiles of foreign influence (I conjure you to believe me, fellow-citizens) the jealousy of a free people ought to be *constantly* awake; since history and experience prove that foreign influence is one of the most baneful foes of Republican Government. But that jealousy to be useful must be impartial; else it becomes the instrument of the very influence to be avoided, instead of a defence against it.

Excessive partiality for one foreign nation, and excessive dislike for another, cause those whom they actuate to see danger only on one side, and serve to veil and even second the arts of influence of the other.—Real patriots, who may resist the intrigues of the favourite, are liable to become suspected and odious; while its tools and dupes usurp the applause and confidence of the people, to surrender their interests.

The great rule of conduct for us, in regard to foreign nations, is in extending our commercial relations, to have with them as little *political* connection as possible. So far as we have already formed engagements, let them be fulfilled with perfect good faith.—Here let us stop.

Europe has a set of primary interests, which to us have none, or a very remote relation. Hence she must be engaged in frequent controversies, the causes of which are essentially for foreign to our concerns. Hence, therefore, it must be unwise in us to implicate ourselves, by artificial ties, in the ordinary vicissitudes of her politics, or the ordinary combinations and collisions of her friendships, or enmities.

Our detached and distant situation invites and enables us to pursue a different course. If we remain one people, under an efficient government, the period is not far off, when we may defy material injury from external annoyance; when we may take such an attitude as will cause the neutrality, we may at any time resolve upon, to be scrupulously respected; when belligerent nations, under the impossibility of making acquisitions upon us, will not lightly hazard the giving us provocation; when we may choose peace or war, as our interest, guided by justice, shall counsel.

Why forego the advantages of so peculiar a situation? Why quit our own to stand upon foreign ground? Why, by interweaving our destiny with that of any part of Europe, entangle our peace and prosperity in the toils of European ambition, rivalship, interest, humour or caprice?

'Tis our true policy to steer clear of permanent alliances, with any portion of the foreign world; so far, I mean, as we are now at liberty to do it; for let me not be understood as capable of patronising infidelity to existing engagements. I hold the maxim no less applicable to public than to private affairs, that honesty is always the best policy. I repeat it, therefore, let those engagements be observed in their genuine sense. But in my opinion, it is unnecessary and would be unwise to extend them.

Taking care always to keep ourselves, by suitable establishments, on a respectable defensive posture, we may safely trust to temporary alliances for extraordinary emergencies.

Harmony, liberal intercourse with all nations, are recommended by policy, humanity, and interest. But even our commercial policy should hold an equal and impartial hand; neither seeking nor granting exclusive favours or preferences; consulting the natural course of things; diffusing and diversifying by gentle means the streams of commerce, but forcing nothing; establishing, with powers so disposed, in order to give trade a liable course, to define the rights of our merchants, and to enable the government to support them; conventional rules of intercourse, the best that present circumstances and mutual opinion will permit, but temporary, and liable to be from time to time abandoned or varied, as experience and circumstances shall dictate; constantly keeping in view,

 that 'tis folly in one nation to look for disinterested favours from another; that it must pay with a portion of its independence for whatever it may accept under that character; that by such acceptance, it may place itself in the condition of having given equivalents for nominal favours, and yet of being reproached with ingratitude for not giving more. There can be no greater error than to expect, or calculate upon real favours from nation to nation. 'Tis an illusion which experience must cure, which a just pride ought to discard.

In offering to you, my countrymen, these counsels of an old and affectionate friend, I dare not hope they will make the strong and lasting impression I could wish; that they will controul the usual current of the passions, or prevent our nation from running the course which has hitherto marked the destiny of nations:

But if I may even flatter myself, that they may be productive of some partial benefit, some occasional good; that they may now and then recur to moderate the fury of party spirit, to warn against the mischiefs of foreign intrigue, to guard against the impostures of pretended patriotism; this"

hope will be a full recompence for the solicitude for your welfare, by which they have been dictated.

How far in the discharge of my official duties, I have been guided by the principles which have been delineated, the public records and other evidences of my conduct must witness to you and to the world. To myself, the assurance of my own conscience is, that I have at least believed myself to be guided by them.

In relation to the still subsisting war in Europe, my Proclamation of the 22d of April 1793 is the index to my Plan. Sanctioned by your approving voice and by that of your Representatives in both Houses of Congress, the spirit of that measure has continually governed me; uninfluenced by any attempts to deter or divert me from it.

After deliberate examination with the aid of the best lights I could obtain, I was well satisfied that our country, under all the circumstances of the case, had a right to take, and was bound in duty and interest, to take a neutral position. Having taken it, I determined, as far as should depend upon me, to maintain it, with moderation, perseverance and firmness.

The considerations which respect the right to hold this conduct, it is not necessary on this occasion to detail. I will only observe, that according to my understanding of the matter, that right, so far from being denied by any of the Belligerent Powers, has been virtually admitted by all.

The duty of holding a neutral conduct may be inferred, without any thing more, from the obligation which justice and humanity impose on every nation, in cases in which it is free to act, to maintain inviolate the relations of peace and amity towards other nations.

The inducements of interest for observing that conduct will best be referred to your own reflections and experience. With me, a predominant motive has been to endeavour to gain time to our country to settle and mature its yet recent institutions, and to progress without interruption, to that degree of strength and consistency, which is necessary to give it, humanly speaking, the command of its own fortunes

"Though in reviewing the incidents of my administration, I am unconscious of intentional error: I am nevertheless too sensible of my defects not to think it probable that I may have committed many errors. Whatever they may be I fervently beseech the Almighty to avert or mitigate the evils to which they may tend. I shall also carry with me the hope that my Country will never cease to view them with indulgence; and that after forty-five years of my life dedicated to its service, with an upright zeal, the faults of incompetent abilities will be consigned to oblivion, as myself must soon be to the mansions of rest.

Relying on its kindness in this as in other things, and actuated by that fervent love towards it, which is so natural to a man, who views in it the native soil of himself and his progenitors for several generations; I anticipate with pleasing expectation that retreat, in which I promise myself to realize, without alloy, the sweet enjoyment of partaking, in the midst of my fellow Citizens, the benign influence of good laws under a free government—the ever favourite object of my heart, and the happy reward, as I trust, of our mutual cares, labours and dangers."

G. WASHINGTON

OUR HOPE

If we cannot freely speak of our beliefs in God or whichever way we choose to worship, then how should we worship our Heavenly Father?

George Washington proclaimed to The Baptist Churches of Virginia in May 1789:
"I beg you will be persuaded that no one would be more zealous than myself to establish effectual barriers against the horrors of spiritual tyranny, and every species of religious persecution—For you, doubtless, remember that I have often expressed my sentiment, that every man, conducting himself as a good citizen, and being accountable to God alone for his religious opinions, ought to be protected in worshipping the Deity according to the dictates of his own conscience."

GW also said to Mary Ball Washington regarding the mind on February 15,1787:
"For happiness depends more upon the internal frame of a persons own mind-than on the externals of the world."

George Washington was an Anglican Christian. He also was a Freemason. In regard to this, in this chapter I will be using a lot of King James Bible verses for such a sensitive topic that we will be talking about. Which is the falling asleep, passing away or death of people we know, love or hear about.

There are copious amounts of things that people pass away from in 2020. Heart disease is still the number one cause of death in the United States today. Next there are other diseases like cancer that take many lives. Car collisions is a big one and so is drug overdose with opioids. Now this is not a formative list. The things that I have named are just a few major contenders. Suicide is a big one too, whether that is by intentionally walking in front of a vehicle, using a firearm, poison, or hanging. It's very sad. Makes you stop and think to be thankful for what you have and to be alive, doesn't it?

If you are not a Christian or even if you are, remember that George Washington was and his belief in God was deep and passionate. President Washington saw the worst in humanity and changed his heart on many things. Furthermore as you read these verses remember that George possibly, (it's not proven), could have read these before or used these before in times such as this topic covers on the passing away of individuals.

Where does your mind go when someone you know or look up to passes away? Does your mind go to God's Word or your moral compass to focus and comfort you? All the individuals present at the passing away of George Washington could have gone to their moral compass or Godly beliefs for comfort. But there is no way to know for sure if those people did.

When the rocky waves of life come crashing in sometimes it is possible to let those hurricane storms reside for a just moment. But thoughts of sadness have to leave because they cannot give us true comfort. Those thoughts are like a tide. They come and they go. We push back those thoughts of sadness like a rescinding tide with God's Word or our moral compass or our beliefs. Life is not easy. But the thing to remember is to not give up. REMEMBER that you are loved and have friends, and family that care for your every need.

1 Thessalonians 4:13-18
v.13 But I would not have you to be ignorant, brethren, concerning them which are asleep, that ye sorrow not, even as others which have no hope.
v.14 For if we believe that Jesus died and rose again, even so them also which sleep in Jesus will God bring with him.
v.15 For this we say unto you by the word of the Lord, that we which are alive and remain unto the coming of the Lord shall not prevent them which are asleep.
v.16 For the Lord himself shall descend from heaven with a shout, with the voice of the archangel, and with the trump of God: and the dead in Christ shall rise first:

v.17 Then we which are alive and remain shall be caught up together with them in the clouds, to meet the Lord in the air: and so shall we ever be with the Lord.
v.18 Wherefore comfort one another with these words.

- God does not want his people to pass away:
  Psalms 116:15 Precious in the sight of the LORD is the death of his saints.

- As sad and precious as it is when someone we know or love passes away there is no conciseness in the grave. Do you think it is fair for some people to see God before we do? God is not a respecter of persons, but of believing:

  Romans 2:11 For there is no respect of persons with God.

  Ephesians 6:9 And, ye masters, do the same things unto them, forbearing threatening:knowing that your Master also is in heaven; neither is there respect of persons with
   him.

  Psalms 6:5 For in death there is no remembrance of thee: in the grave who shall give thee thanks?

  Ecclesiastes 9:10 Whatsoever thy hand findeth to do, do it with thy might; for there is no work, nor device, nor knowledge, nor wisdom, in the grave, whither thou goest.

- God is not the author of death, for that is the devil:
  John 10:10 The thief cometh not, but for to steal, and to kill, and to destroy: I am come that they might have life, and that they might have it more abundantly.

  Hebrews 2:14 Forasmuch then as the children are partakers of flesh and blood, he also himself likewise took part of the same; that through death he might destroy him that had the power of death, that is, the devil;

If you're wondering why there are numerous King James Version bible verses in this George Washington biography, it is because very few Washington biographies show what biblical verses George and Martha possibly could have read delineating a situation at hand. So because George was an Angelicin Christian I decided to put all these verses in this book to bring some kind of comfort about OUR HOPE because in a moment I will be explaining the painful death and passing away of George Washington.

1 Corinthians 15:51-58
v.51 Behold, I shew you a mystery; We shall not all sleep, but we shall all be changed,
v.52 In a moment, in the twinkling of an eye, at the last trump: for the trumpet shall sound, and the dead shall be raised incorruptible, and we shall be changed.
v.53 For this corruptible must put on incorruption, and this mortal must put on immortality.
v.54 So when this corruptible shall have put on incorruption, and this mortal shall have put on immortality, then shall be brought to pass the saying that is written, Death is swallowed up in victory.
v.55 O death, where is thy sting? O grave, where is thy victory?
v.56 The sting of death is sin; and the strength of sin is the law.
v.57 But thanks be to God, which giveth us the victory through our Lord Jesus Christ.
v.58 Therefore, my beloved brethren, be ye stedfast, unmoveable, always abounding in the work of the Lord, forasmuch as ye know that your labour is not in vain in the Lord.

When we hear of some one passing away or we have thoughts of despair, depression or we pontificate our life, "we must not forget that we do not live down in the valley of the wilderness of the world. We look down from the heavenlies as our Heavenly Father's very own…doing his business. We bring light into any room because light is our natural environment. We will never live suppressed in the world but we shall demonstrate God's power as we but live valiantly in our moral compass or our spiritual beliefs." D.M.S.

Considering the indubitably sensitive topic when someone that we know or love passes away what do we do and how do we handle those things? George Washington on December 12,1799 went out for a ride to survey and take care of his property. It was snowing and raining as mentioned in his personal journal. He had guests at his home. When he came back inside George did not change his clothes right away he stayed wet and cold from his ride. Extemporaneously that evening after he had dinner, read the newspaper, entertained his guests and then eventually went to bed, he developed a sore throat. Soon after George and Martha went to bed, in the middle of the night he woke up Martha and was complaining to her about the soreness of his throat getting worse.

Some biographers have said the hoarseness in his throat was getting very rough. Martha wanted to call a doctor and wanted George to take some medicine. George declined and waited till the morning around dawn. Mind you, it was still very cold outside. In the morning George's throat had gotten worse. Martha sent for Dr. Craik, George's personal physician. Dr Craik lived in Alexandria, which was far from Mount Vernon. George's throat condition was severe and deteriorating. In the mean time Martha summoned Dr. Gustavus Brown and Dr. Elijah Dick who lived nearby and came to George's bedside.

What was happening after George had been outside in the cold and after being in his wet clothes for so long is that our beloved George Washington at sixty seven years of age had developed what you could say was acute tonsillitis or the inflammation of his tonsils. Those three doctors agreed what George had was "quincy". Quincy basically was a tightening or swelling of the windpipe. He couldn't breathe. The windpipe got smaller and smaller. Kind of like suffocation. It is a pretty terrible way to pass away.

You would not want to see your loved one or people you look up to pass away in that manner. It's very sad but in George Washington's time and culture with the medical knowledge available the doctors thought they were doing good taking up to five liters of blood from him through a process known as bloodletting. Also, they had a concoction of molasses, vinegar and butter to soothe his throat. But in attempting to drink this, Washington almost suffocated because of his deteriorating condition. One of the doctors suggested a new procedure that we know today as a tracheotomy. A tracheotomy is a slit or tiny air hole that was to be placed in George's throat to unblock his airway. Dr. Craik, George's personal physician, said no to the tracheotomy. Dr. Craik was so sure and stubborn of his medical expertise that he would save Washington, but his expertise did not. His beloved beautiful wife Martha was there the whole time. One of GW's most trusted companions, Tobias Lear his personal secretary, took to his diary of George's situation.

More people that were by George's bedside were Christopher Sheels, and Molly, and Charlotte and Caroline. These fine people were servants or slaves of the Washington estate. They were part of a dowry that was issued by Martha's first marriage of a different estate. So when George Washington freed his slaves in his will it was only a portion of those individuals because of Virginia law that was deeply rooted in British roots of the international slave trade. George wanted in his will wanted to free all of his slaves but he couldn't because of Virginia law. In the process of all this going on, knowing that he is about to go or pass away he asks his beloved wife to get the two wills he had written. George has her burn one to ash and to keep the other one that freed his slaves. George changed his heart on many things. He along with others laid the foundation of freedom for liberty and justice for all. Though not perfect, The Constitution of the United States and it's citizens within 100 years abolishes slavery after the Founding documents were written.

Dr. Craik was speaking with George, and George told him that "I die hard but I am not afraid to go". Later George was speaking to someone in the room and he said "tis well". Those were the last words ever spoken by POTUS1. Washington was afraid of being buried alive. So he asked in his will not to be buried until three days after he passed away. Tobias Lear made sure of that happening. So four days after GW passed away they buried him. Also one of the most famous eulogies for George Washington was by one of GW's most trusted soldiers from the battlefield, Light Horse Harry Lee. Light Horse Harry was the father who we know today as Robert E. Lee. The words of the eulogy by Harry Lee were "First in war, first in peace, first in the hearts of his countrymen"

This is George Washington.

This is POTUS1.

REFERENCE NOTES:

Adams, John:

https://www.mountvernon.org/library/digitalhistory/digital-encyclopedia/article/john-adams/

Alexander Hamilton:

https://www.mountvernon.org/library/digitalhistory/digital-encyclopedia/article/alexander-hamilton/

Benjamin Franklin:

https://www.mountvernon.org/library/digitalhistory/digital-encyclopedia/article/benjamin-franklin/

Bestiality:

https://www.britannica.com/topic/zoophilia

https://m.huffpost.com/us/entry/us_57a3b150e4b021fd987816d8

https://www.independent.co.uk/news/world/americas/sex-animals-men-jailed-horses-farm-bestiality-munson-pennsylvania-a8883601.html

Black soldiers during the revolution:

https://www.army.mil/article/97705/black_soldiers_in_the_revolutionary_war

Bill of Rights Ratified:

https://www.mountvernon.org/education/primary-sources-2/article/united-states-bill-of-rights/

https://www.history.com/this-day-in-history/bill-of-rights-passes-congress

Charlottesville Riot, Full Transcript of President Trump:

https://www.latimes.com/politics/la-na-pol-trump-charlottesville-transcript-20170815-story.html

https://www.nationalreview.com/2017/08/trump-blame-both-sides-charlottesville-statement-factual-correct-description-trump/

Cars/transportation:

https://www.asirt.org/safe-travel/road-safety-facts/

https://www.driverknowledge.com/car-accident-statistics/

Civil Right Act of 1964/1965:

https://www.archives.gov/education/lessons/civil-rights-act

https://www.ourdocuments.gov/doc.php?flash=false&doc=100

https://youtu.be/Vm4ZCzzX7Sw

Civil Rights Act of 1875:

https://www.senate.gov/artandhistory/history/common/generic/CivilRightsAct1875.htm

Coinage act of 1792:

https://www.usmint.gov/learn/history/historical-documents/coinage-act-of-april-2-1792

Copyright Law:

https://www.copyright.gov/about/1790-copyright-act.html

Disease/injuries:

https://www.medicalnewstoday.com/articles/282929.php

https://www.cdc.gov/nchs/fastats/leading-causes-of-death.htm

https://www.advisory.com/daily-briefing/2019/01/16/deaths

https://afsp.org/about-suicide/suicide-statistics/

Draft to the Declaration of Independence:

https://www.blackpast.org/african-american-history/declaration-independence-and-debate-over-slavery/

Drugs/alcohol:

https://www.cdc.gov/drugoverdose/data/statedeaths.html

https://www.cdc.gov/vitalsigns/alcohol-poisoning-deaths/index.htm

Established Capitol along Potomac River and to be called the District of Columbia:

https://www.politico.com/story/2017/07/16/president-washington-signs-residence-act-july-16-1790-240468

https://www.mountvernon.org/education/primary-sources-2/article/residence-act-of-1790/

Ecosex:

https://www.mandatory.com/fun/1400975-folks-believe-sex-nature-save/amp#referrer=https%3A%2F%2F

www.google.com&_tf=From%20%251%24s

https://www.vice.com/en_us/article/wdbgyq/ecosexuals-believe-having-sex-with-the-earth-could-save-it

Farewell Address:

"Farewell Address, 19 September 1796," *Founders Online,* National Archives, https://founders.archives.gov/documents/Washington/99-01-02-00963.

Firearms:

"A Defence of the Constitutions of Government". Book by John Adams. Chapter 3: "Marchamont Nedham: Errors of Government and Rules of Policy", Sixth Rule, 1787.

http://hua.umf.maine.edu/Reading_Revolutions/Adams.html

https://www.pewresearch.org/fact-tank/2019/08/16/what-the-data-says-about-gun-deaths-in-the-u-s/

https://lawcenter.giffords.org/facts/gun-violence-statistics/#state

https://www.bradyunited.org/key-statistics

https://everytownresearch.org/gun-violence-america/

https://www.youtube.com/watch?v=TyXcY7NJHFg

https://www.youtube.com/watch?v=X6J7j82PCWI

https://www.prageru.com/video/what-should-we-do-about-guns/

https://www.prageru.com/video/gun-rights-are-womens-rights/

https://www.merriam-webster.com/dictionary/discipline

Heritage Guide to the Constitution by Edwin Meese III on pages 318-322

America's Constitution by Akhil Reed Amar pages 321-325
"Hands Off My Gun" by Dana Loesch

https://www.nraila.org/get-the-facts/second-amendment-right-to-keep-and-bear-arms/

https://www.nraila.org/get-the-facts/assault-weapons-large-magazines/

https://www.nraila.org/get-the-facts/handguns/

https://www.nraila.org/articles/20191021/confiscation-or-mandatory-buyback

https://www.washingtontimes.com/news/2017/apr/12/second-amendment-protects-the-assault-rifles/

https://www.washingtontimes.com/news/2013/jan/10/the-right-to-shoot-tyrants-not-deer/

https://www.washingtonpost.com/opinions/repealing-the-second-amendment-is-a-dangerous-idea/2018/03/28/ab194138-32af-11e8-8bdd-cdb33a5eef83_story.html

https://www.washingtonpost.com/blogs/post-partisan/wp/2018/03/28/repealing-the-second-amendment-would-be-incredibly-difficult/

First revenue law, the whiskey tax:

https://history.house.gov/Historical-Highlights/1700s/The-1791-Excise-Whiskey-Tax/

https://www2.gwu.edu/~ffcp/exhibit/p14/p14_6.html

Fugitive Slave Act (this was superseded by the 13th amendment) :

https://www.politico.com/story/2014/02/this-day-in-politics-congress-enacts-first-fugitive-slave-law-feb-12-1793-103375

https://www.mountvernon.org/education/primary-sources-2/article/fugitive-slave-act-of-1793/

https://constitutioncenter.org/interactive-constitution/amendment/amendment-xiii

Funding act to assume all Revolutionary war debt from states:

https://en.wikipedia.org/wiki/Funding_Act_of_1790

https://www.britannica.com/biography/Alexander-Hamilton-United-States-statesman/Hamiltons-financial-program

God and George Washington:

"Washington's God" by Michael and Jana Novak pages 19, 21, 96-101, 116-118, 122, 125,128, 147-149, 235,237-242

Letter from George Washington to Edward Newenham October 20, 1792

"Praying with the Presidents" by Ron Dicianni

"The Heritage Guide to the Constitution" by Edwin Meese III, Matthew Spalding, & David Forte on pages 307-311

"America's Constitution" by Akhil Reed Amar pages 315-320

Letter from Thomas Jefferson to the Danbury Baptists about a figurative wall of separation of church and state.

https://www.loc.gov/loc/lcib/9806/danpre.html

https://www.constitution.org/tj/sep_church_state.htm

Hemp:

"First Entrepreneur" by Edward Lengel pages 60 and 69

https://www.mountvernon.org/george-washington/facts/george-washington-grew-hemp/

Human/Sex Trafficking of today:

https://www.whitehouse.gov/briefings-statements/president-donald-j-trump-taking-action-end-human-trafficking/

https://www.whitehouse.gov/briefings-statements/president-donald-j-trump-fighting-eradicate-human-trafficking/

https://www.whitehouse.gov/presidential-actions/executive-order-combating-human-trafficking-online-child-exploitation-united-states/

https://www.state.gov/reports/2020-trafficking-in-persons-report/

https://obamawhitehouse.archives.gov/the-press-office/2012/09/25/fact-sheet-obama-administration-announces-efforts-combat-human-trafficki

https://www.foxnews.com/us/anti-trafficking-leader-praises-ice-trump

https://www.ice.gov/features/human-trafficking

https://www.dhs.gov/blue-campaign/what-human-trafficking

https://fortune.com/2019/04/14/human-sex-trafficking-us-slavery/

http://cup.columbia.edu/book/sex-trafficking-in-the-united-states/9780231172639

https://dailycaller.com/2019/08/16/trump-sex-trafficking-jaco-booyens/

https://www.dailymail.co.uk/news/article-4745938/Slavery-profitable-experts-warn.html

https://www.theepochtimes.com/breaking-down-the-alarming-realities-of-child-sex-trafficking-in-america-jaco-booyens_3207498.html

https://www.theepochtimes.com/trump-creates-new-position-dedicated-to-fighting-human-trafficking_3223105.html

https://www.humanrightscareers.com/issues/human-trafficking-books/

Human trafficking/Pizzagate:

https://www.thelastamericanvagabond.com/13-essential-data-points-pizzagate-pedophilia-allegations/

https://www.snopes.com/fact-check/pizzagate-conspiracy/

https://www.breitbart.com/politics/2020/09/21/report-u-s-virgin-islands-ag-requests-jeffrey-epstein-flight-logs/

Homosexuality:

https://www.theguardian.com/technology/2018/nov/29/grindr-apps-president-calls-marriage-holy-matrimony-between-man-and-woman

https://metro.co.uk/2016/12/22/father-and-son-allowed-to-marry-6339373/

https://www.rga.com/work/case-studies/love-labels

https://www.amazon.com/George-Washingtons-Rules-Live-Manners/dp/1426315007

https://www.focusonthefamily.com/socialissues/marriage/marriage/the-foundation-of-marriage

https://www.frc.org/brochure/the-bibles-teaching-on-marriage-and-family

https://www.heritage.org/marriage-and-family/report/the-necessity-marriage

Jay, John:

https://www.mountvernon.org/library/digitalhistory/digital-encyclopedia/article/john-jay/

Jay's Treaty:

"Mr. President" by Harlow Giles Unger pages 209-217

"Washington: The Indispensable Man" by James Thomas Flexner (illustrated edition) pages 337-342

https://www.mountvernon.org/library/digitalhistory/digital-encyclopedia/article/jay-treaty/

JFK executive order 10925:

 http://www.oeod.uci.edu/policies/aa_history.php

Judiciary Act of 1789:

https://www.supremecourthistory.org/

https://www.loc.gov/rr/program/bib/ourdocs/judiciary.html

https://www.fjc.gov/history/timeline/judiciary-act-1789-defines-jurisdiction-federal-courts

https://www.ourdocuments.gov/doc.php?flash=false&doc=12

Kentucky:

https://www.history.com/topics/us-states/kentucky

Knifes:

 https://www.lawenforcementtoday.com/fbi-more-people-killed-with-knives-hammers-clubs-and-even-feet-than-rifles-in-2018/

Laws passed by POTUS1:

https://www.mountvernon.org/george-washington/the-first-president/inauguration/timeline/

https://www.mountvernon.org/education/primary-sources-2/type/legislation/

https://www.mountvernon.org/george-washington/the-first-president/ten-facts-about-washingtons-presidency/

https://millercenter.org/president/george-washington/key-events

https://www.thoughtco.com/foreign-policy-under-george-washington-3310346

Mass shootings statistics:

https://fortune.com/2018/07/03/us-mass-shootings-1949-2018/

https://www.psychologytoday.com/us/blog/evolutionary-politics/201908/are-mass-shootings-becoming-more-common

http://behindthetower.org/a-brief-history-of-mass-shootings

Militia Act:

https://www.mountvernon.org/education/primary-sources-2/article/militia-act-of-1792/

https://www.history.com/this-day-in-history/militia-act-establishes-conscription-under-federal-law

Moratorium on International Slave trade:

https://www.youtube.com/watch?v=Ck19M3Zy864&list=PLr40fFkNNADFoXZi78o9951CxOkjk2I1p&index=22

National Bank established:

https://history.house.gov/Historical-Highlights/1700s/1791_First_Bank/

https://www.mountvernon.org/education/primary-sources-2/article/first-bank-of-the-united-states/

Naturalization Acts of 1790 & 1795:

https://www.mountvernon.org/education/primary-sources-2/article/naturalization-acts-of-1790-and-1795/

Naval Act (establishes navy):

https://www.history.navy.mil/browse-by-topic/heritage/origins-of-the-navy/washington-naval-act-1794.html

Neutrality Acts 4/22/1793:

https://www.mountvernon.org/library/digitalhistory/digital-encyclopedia/article/neutrality-proclamation/

North Carolina :
https://www.loc.gov/item/today-in-history/november-21/

Race:

https://www.newsmax.com/thewire/worst-run-cities-united-states/2019/07/15/id/924463/

https://www.investors.com/politics/editorials/worst-run-states-big-spending-democrats/

https://amac.us/americas-25-worst-cities-are-democrat-led-the-answer-new-leaders/

https://www.realclearpolitics.com/articles/2020/06/17/a_backlash_against_democratic_control_of_cities__143474.html

https://www.usatoday.com/story/opinion/2020/07/03/police-black-killings-homicide-rates-race-injustice-column/3235072001/

https://www.usatoday.com/story/news/factcheck/2020/06/23/fact-check-how-many-unarmed-black-men-did-police-kill-2019/5322455002/

https://fatherhoodfactor.com/us-fatherless-statistics/

https://www.fatherhood.org/father-absence-statistic

https://www.pewsocialtrends.org/2015/12/17/1-the-american-family-today/

https://www.childtrends.org/publications/dramatic-increase-in-percentage-of-births-outside-marriage-among-whites-hispanics-and-women-with-higher-education-levels

https://www.pewsocialtrends.org/2018/04/25/the-changing-profile-of-unmarried-parents/

https://www.nationalreview.com/2000/06/black-black-silence-deroy-murdock/

http://walterewilliams.com/kanye-and-democrats/

https://www.nationalreview.com/2018/05/black-republicans-uncle-tom-card-dead/

The Rainbow:

https://en.wikipedia.org/wiki/Rainbow#Culture

https://www.britannica.com/story/how-did-the-rainbow-flag-become-a-symbol-of-lgbt-pride

https://biblefocus.net/consider/v20rainbow/index.html

https://answersingenesis.org/the-flood/taking-back-the-rainbow/

https://slate.com/human-interest/2012/06/supreme-court-doma-decision-why-is-the-rainbow-a-symbol-of-gay-marriage.html

Rhode Island:

https://avalon.law.yale.edu/18th_century/ratri.asp

Slavery:

"Extraordinary, Ordinary People" by Condolezza Rice page 157
"The Only Unavoidable Subject of Regret" by Mary V. Thompson page 329

 "The Indian World of George Washington" by Colin G. Calloway page 492

https://www.heritage.org/progressivism/commentary/the-1619-projects-outrageous-lying-slander-abe-lincoln

https://www.heritage.org/american-founders/commentary/1776-not-1619

https://www.washingtontimes.com/news/2020/may/24/editorial-1619-project-bad-history-fueled-bad-moti/

Slavery/enslaved community at Mount Vernon:

https://www.youtube.com/watch?v=1iRR5SmJaJA&list=PLr40fFk NNADFoXZi78o9951CxOkjk2l1p&index=21

 https://www.mountvernon.org/george-washington/slavery/ten-facts-about-washington-slavery/

https://www.mountvernon.org/george-washington/slavery/

https://www.youtube.com/watch?v=7bSMskfNZNw

Slave Trade Act of 1794:

https://youtu.be/Ck19M3Zy864

http://abolition.nypl.org/essays/us_constitution/4/

https://www.revolvy.com/page/Slave-Trade-Act-of-1794

https://history.house.gov/Exhibitions-and-Publications/BAIC/Historical-Data/Constitutional-Amendments-and-Legislation/

https://www.mountvernon.org/education/primary-sources-2/article/slave-trade-act-of-1794/

https://www.loc.gov/law/help/statutes-at-large/3rd-congress/session-1/c3s1ch11.pdf

https://www.docsteach.org/documents/document/slave-trade-act-1794

https://www.archives.gov/education/lessons/slave-trade.html

States rights:
The Heritage Guide to the Constitution" by Edwin Meese III, Matthew Spalding, David Forte on pages (366-374)

"America's Constitution: a biography" by Akhil reed Amar, pages (321-329)

https://www.mountvernon.org/george-washington/constitutional-convention/6-key-players-at-the-constitutional-convention/

November 9, 1787 George Washington to Bushrod Washington on the power of the constitution being to the people and states.

https://founders.archives.gov/gewn-04-05-02-0388

State of The Union Address January 8, 1790:

https://www.mountvernon.org/education/primary-sources/state-of-the-union-address/
https://founders.archives.gov/documents/Washington/05-04-02-0361

Suicide:

https://suicidepreventionlifeline.org/

https://www. afsp.org/suicide-statistics/

https://www.nimh.nih.gov/health/statistics/suicide.shtml

https://www.who.int/mental_health/prevention/suicide/suicideprevent/en/

https://www.cdc.gov/nchs/fastats/suicide.htm

https://www.va.gov/health-care/health-needs-conditions/mental-health/suicide-prevention/

https://en.wikipedia.org/wiki/History_of_suicide

https://www.statista.com/statistics/187478/death-rate-from-suicide-in-the-us-by-gender-since-1950/

Tariff Act of 1789:

https://en.wikipedia.org/wiki/Tariff_of_1789

Tennessee:

https://www.politico.com/story/2016/06/tennessee-enters-union-june-1-1796-223706

https://sos.tn.gov/products/tennessee-state-constitution

https://www.census.gov/history/www/through_the_decades/fast_f
acts/1790_fast_facts.html

The year 1883 :

https://www.thoughtco.com/1883-civil-rights-cases-4134310

**Time and Manner of Administrating certain oaths (First act
of Congress):**

https://prologue.blogs.archives.gov/2014/05/30/the-oath-of-
office-the-first-act-of-the-first-congress/

Treaty of San Lorenzo:

https://www.mountvernon.org/education/primary-sources-
2/article/pinckneys-treaty/

https://history.state.gov/milestones/1784-1800/pickney-treaty

Treaty of Tripoli:

https://avalon.law.yale.edu/18th_century/bar1796n.asp

https://www.loc.gov/law/help/us-treaties/bevans/b-tripoli-
ust000011-1070.pdf

Trump Impeachment:

https://www.businessinsider.com/list-of-impeached-us-
presidents-2019-12?r=US&IR=T

https://www.breitbart.com/politics/2020/10/06/declassified-cia-
documents-reveal-brennan-briefed-obama-on-clintons-plan-to-
tie-trump-to-russia/

https://www.washingtontimes.com/news/2020/feb/5/donald-
trump-acquitted-senate-impeachment-trial/

https://www.foxnews.com/opinion/russia-hoax-lie-hillary-clinton-gregg-jarrett

https://history.com/this-day-in-history/president-trump-impeached-house-of-representatives

https://www.cnn.com/specials/politics/trump-impeachment

https://www.usatoday.com/story/news/politics/2020/02/05/impeachment-after-trump-acquittal-slew-investigations-lawsuits/4620766002/

Vermont:

https://www.history.com/topics/us-states/vermont

Whiskey Rebellion:

"Mr. President" by Harlow Giles Unger pages 133-147 & 183-197

"Washington: The Indispensable Man" by James Thomas Flexner (illustrated edition) pages 325-330

https://www.mountvernon.org/library/digitalhistory/digital-encyclopedia/article/whiskey-rebellion/

11th Amendment:

https://www.loc.gov/rr/program/bib/ourdocs/judiciary.html

https://www.britannica.com/topic/Eleventh-Amendment

3/5 compromise:
"The Heritage Guide to the Constitution" by Edwin Meese III, Matthew Spalding, David Forte on pages 54-56

https://www.prageru.com/video/why-the-threefifths-compromise-was-anti-slavery/

13/14/15th amendments:

"The Heritage Guide to the Constitution" by Edwin Meese III, Matthew Spalding, David Forte on pages 380-411

1st Naturalization Law (established terms of citizenship, according to the culture of that time):

https://www.encyclopedia.com/social-sciences/encyclopedias-almanacs-transcripts-and-maps/act-march-26-1790

https://www.mountvernon.org/education/primary-sources-2/article/naturalization-acts-of-1790-and-1795/

2nd amendment:

https://www.archives.gov/federal-register/constitution

BIBLIOGRAPHY

Allen, Thomas B., and Cheryl Harness. *George Washington, Spymaster: How America Outspied the British and Won the Revolutionary War*. National Geographic, 2004.

Avlon, John P. Washington's Farewell: the Founding Father's Warning to Future Generations. Simon & Schuster, 2017.

Beck, Glenn, and Kevin Balfe. Being George Washington: the Indispensable Man, as You've Never Seen Him. Threshold Editions/Mercury Radio Arts, 2012.

Beck, Glenn, et al. *Arguing with Socialists*. Threshold Editions/Mercury Radio Arts, an Imprint of Simon & Schuster, Inc., 2020.

Brady, Patricia. *Martha Washington: an American Life*. Penguin Books, 2006.

Breen, T. H. *George Washington's Journey: The President Forges a New Nation*. Simon & Schuster, 2017.

Brookhiser, Richard. *Founding Father*. Simon & Schuster, 1997.

Bullinger, E W. Commentary on Revelation, or The Apocalypse . Adansonia Publishing, 2018.

Bullinger, E W. The Church Epistles: Romans to Thessalonians. Cosimo Classics, 1905.

Bullinger, E W. The Companion Bible: The Authorized Version of 1611 with the Structures and Critical, Explanatory, and Suggestive Notes and with 198 Appendixes. Kregel Publications, 1990.

Burns, James MacGregor., and Susan Dunn. *George Washington*. Times Books, 2004.

Calloway, Colin G. *The Indian World of George Washington: the First President, the First Americans, and the Birth of the Nation*. Oxford University Press, 2019.

Charen, Mona. Sex Matters: How Modern Feminism Lost Touch with Science, Love, and Common Sense. Crown Forum, 2018.

Chernow, Ron. *Washington: a Life*. Penguin Books, 2011.

Coe, Alexis. You Never Forget Your First: A Biography of George Washington. Penguin Books, 2020.

Coolidge, Calvin, and Peter Hannaford. *The Quotable Calvin Coolidge: Sensible Words for a New Century*. Images from the Past, 2013.

Clinton, Bill. *My Life*. Hutchinson, 2004.

Day, Vox. SJWS Always Lie: Taking down the Thought Police. Castalia House, 2015.

Dershowitz, Alan. *The Case for Israel*. John Wiley & Sons, Inc., 2011.

D'Souza, Dinesh. *United States of Socialism: Who's behind It. Why It's Evil. How to Stop It*. All Points Books, an Imprint of St. Martin's Publishing Group, 2020.

D'Souza, Dinesh. *The Roots of Obama's Rage*. Regnery, 2011.

Earhardt, Ainsley, and Mark A. Tabb. *The Light within Me: an Inspirational Memoir*. Harper, an Imprint of Harper Collins Publishers, 2018.

Ellis, Joseph J. *His Excellency: George Washington*. Alfred A. Knopf, 2011.

Flexner, James Thomas. *Washington: the Indispensable Man*. Collins, 1976.

George Washington's Mount Vernon: Official Guidebook. Mount Vernon Ladies' Association, 2017.

Hagopian, Joachim. Pedophilia & Empire: Satan, Sodomy, and the Deep State: Book 4 (North America's Shameful Pedophilia Scandals Like Never Before. Independently Published , 2020.

Haley, Nikki R. *With all due respect: Defending America with Grit and Grace*. St.Martin's Press, 2019.

Hamilton, Alexander, et al. The Federalist. Barnes & Noble Books, 2004.

Hanson, Victor Davis. *The Case for Trump*. Basic Books, 2019.

Hanson, Victor Davis. The Dying Citizen: How Progressive Elites, Tribalism, and Globalization Are Destroying the Idea of America. Basic Books, 2021.

Heidler, David S., and Jeanne T. Heidler. *Washington's Circle: the Creation of the President*. Random House, 2016.

Henriques, Peter R. *Realistic Visionary: a Portrait of George Washington*. University of Virginia Press, 2006.

Henriques, Peter R. First and Always: A New Portrait of George Washington. University of Virginia Press, 2020.

Horn, Jonathan. Washington's End: The Final Years and Forgotten Struggle. Scribner, 2020.

Humphreys, David, et al. David Humphreys' Life of General Washington: With George Washington's "Remarks". University of Georgia Press, 2006.

Johnson, Paul. *George Washington: the Founding Father*. Harper Perennial, 2005.

Kapp, Friedrich *The Life of Frederick William Von Steuben, Major General In the Revolutionary Army*, 1859

Keene, David A., and Thomas L. Mason. Shall Not Be Infringed: The New Assaults on Your Second Amendment. Skyhorse Publishing, 2016.

Kengor, Paul. *The Politically Incorrect Guide to Communism*. Regnery Publishing, 2017.

Kennedy, Robert Francis. The Real Anthony Fauci: Bill Gates, Big Pharma, and the Global War on Democracy and Public Health. Skyhorse Publishing, 2021.

Ketchum, Richard M. *The World of George Washington*. American Heritage Publishing, 1974.

Kesler, Charles R. Crisis of the Two Constitutions: The Rise, Decline, and Recovery of American Greatness. Encounter Books, 2021.

Kilmeade, Brian, and Don Yaeger. *George Washington's Secret Six: the Spy Ring That Saved the American Revolution*. Sentinel, 2013.

Lengel, Edward G. *First Entrepreneur: How George Washington Built His--and the Nation's--Prosperity*. Da Capo Press, a Member of the Perseus Books Group, 2016.

Lengel, Edward G. *Inventing George Washington: America's Founder, in Myth and Memory*. Harper, 2011.

Lengel, Edward G. General George Washington: a Military Life. Random House Trade Paperbacks, 2007.

Lillback, Peter A., and Jerry Newcombe. *George Washington's Sacred Fire*. Providence Forum Press, 2006.

Lott, John R. *The War on Guns: Arming Yourself against Gun Control Lies*. Regnery Publishing, A Division of Salem Media Group, 2016.

Lockhart, Paul Douglas. *The Drillmaster of Valley Forge: the Baron De Steuben and the Making of the American Army*. Harper, 2010.

Lukas, Carrie L. The Politically Incorrect Guide to Women, Sex, and Feminism. Regency Publishing, Inc., an Eagle Publishing Company, 2006.

Madison, James. Notes of Debates in the Federal Convention of 1787. Ohio Univ. Press, 1985.

Meese III, Edwin. The Heritage Guide to the Constitution. Heritage Foundation, 2005.

Novak, Michael, and Jana Novak. *Washington's God: Religion, Liberty, and the Father of Our Country*. A Member of the Perseus Books Group, 2006.

Obama, Barack. *The Audacity of Hope: Thoughts on Reclaiming the American Dream*. Three Rivers Press, 2008.

Owens, Candace. *Blackout: How Black America Can Make Its Second Escape from the Democrat Plantation*. Threshold Editions, an Imprint of Simon & Schuster, Inc., 2020.

Pelton, Robert W. *George Washington's Prayers*. Freedom & Liberty Foundation Press, 2017.
Randall, Willard Sterne. George Washington: A Life. Henry Holt and Company LLC, 1997.

Rhodehamel, John. *George Washington: The Wonder of the Age*. Yale University Press, 2017.

Rice, Condoleezza. *Extraordinary, Ordinary People: a Memoir of Family*. Crown Archetype, 2010.

Rice, Condoleezza. *Democracy: Stories from the Long Road to Freedom*. Twelve, 2017.

Rice, Condoleezza. *No Higher Honor: a Memoir of My Years in Washington*. Crown Publishers, 2011.

Ridley, Jasper. The Freemasons: A History of the World's Most Powerful Secret Society. Skyhorse Publishing, Inc., 2011.

Riley, Naomi Schaefer. The New Trail of Tears: How Washington Is Destroying American Indians. Encounter Books, 2016.

Rogers, Will, and Bryan B. Sterling. The Best of Will Rogers. MJF Books, 1979.

Shlaes, Amity. *Coolidge*. Harper Perennial, 2014.

Shrier, Abigail. Irreversible Damage: The Transgender Craze Seducing Our Daughters. Regnery Publishing, a Division of Salem Media Group, 2021.

Stark, Peter. *Young Washington: How Wilderness and War Forged America's Founding Father*. Ecco, 2018

Tabbert, Mark A. George Washington's Rules for Freemasons in Life and Lodge. Macoy Publishing And Masonic Supply Co. Inc, 2016.

Thompson, Mary V. *"The Only Unavoidable Subject of Regret": George Washington, Slavery, and the Enslaved Community at Mount Vernon*. University of Virginia Press, 2019.

Unger, Harlow G. *"Mr. President": George Washington and the Making of the Nation's Highest Office*. Da Capo Press, 2013.

Unger, Harlow G. *The Unexpected George Washington: His Private Life*. John Wiley & Sons, 2006.

Warren, Jack D., and Anna L. Brownson. *The Presidency of George Washington*. Mount Vernon Ladies' Association, 2000.

Washington, Austin. *The Education of George Washington How a Forgotten Book Shaped the Character of a Hero*. Regnery Publishing, 2014.

Washington, George, and W. B. Allen. George Washington: a Collection. Liberty Fund Inc., 1988.

Washington, George, and Paul M. Zall. *Washington on Washington*. University Press of Kentucky, 2003.

Washington, George. *Quotations of George Washington*. Applewood Books, 2003.

Washington, George. The Journal of Major George Washington: An Account of His First Official Mission, Made as Emissary from the Governor of Virginia to the Commandant of the French Forces on the Ohio, October 1753-January 1754. Colonial Williamsburg Foundation, 1994.

Wheeler, Liz. *Tipping Points: How to Topple the Left's House of Cards*. Regnery Publishing, Incorporated, An Eagle Publishing Company, 2019.

Wiencek, Henry. An Imperfect God George Washington, His Slaves, and the Creation of America. Farrar, Straus and Giroux, 2003.

Wood, Peter W. 1620: A Critical Response to the 1619 Project. Encounter Books, 2020.

Zmirak, John, and Al Perrotta. *The Politically Incorrect Guide to Immigration*. Regnery Publishing, 2018.